# Logic from A to Z

# Logic from A to Z

MICHAEL DETLEFSEN
DAVID CHARLES McCARTY
JOHN B. BACON

London and New York

First published 1999
by Routledge
11 New Fetter Lane, London EC4P 4EE

Simultaneously published in the USA and Canada
by Routledge
29 West 35th Street, New York, NY 10001

*Routledge is an imprint of the Taylor & Francis Group*



Typeset in Times by Routledge
Printed and bound in Great Britain by Clays Ltd, St Ives



*British Library Cataloguing in Publication Data*
A catalogue record for this book is available from
the British Library

*Library of Congress Cataloging in Publication Data*
Applied for

ISBN 0–415–21375–4

# Contents

# Introduction

This book provides students with a glossary of terms used in formal logic and the philosophy of mathematics. The terms include those which will be found in any first course in logic (such as *Argument*, *Truth Table* and *Variable*), those encountered in the study of set and model theory (such as *Isomorphism* and *Function*), computability theory (such as *Algorithm*, *Turing Machine* and *Halting Problem*), and brief statements of some results (such as *Gödels' theorems*, *Herbrand's theorem*, *Löwenheim-Skolem theorem(s)* and *Zorn's lemma*). The book also contains a table of the logical symbols used in set theory, propositional and predicate logic and modal logic.

Entries are organised in alphabetical order. Dummy titles are placed throughout to assist the reader in locating their topic of interest (such as **Effective procedure** *See* Algorithm). Many entries contain cross-references (denoted by italics) to help comprehension or add detail.

# Logic from A to Z

**Abacus machine** *See* Register machine.

**Abstract term** Notion of traditional logic. Signifies a term that names a property. Example: 'wisdom'.

**Abstraction** Term of traditional logic and set theory. In traditional logic it signifies an operation or process whereby one derives a universal from the particulars falling under it. In set theory it signifies the operation or process (also called comprehension) whereby one derives a set as the extension of a property.

*See* Axiom of comprehension; Extension.

***Ad hominem* argument** *See* Argument *ad hominem.*

***Ad ignorantiam* argument** *See* Argument *ad ignorantiam.*

**Adicity** *See* Arity.

**Adjunction** An inference rule in certain systems of formal logic, such as C.I. Lewis' systems for modal logic. The rule of adjunction often takes the form: from the single propositions '*A*' and '*B*' infer the compound proposition '*A* and *B*'.

**Affirmative (proposition)** *See* Categorical proposition.

**Affirming the consequent, fallacy of** Term of logic; a formal fallacy. The fallacy is committed in arguments which, from a conditional premise 'If *A* then *B*' and the assertion of the consequent, *B*, incorrectly conclude the antecedent, *A*.

*See* Conditional, material.

**Alephs** Set-theoretic notation for infinite cardinal numbers, introduced by Cantor in 1893. The first letter of the Hebrew alphabet, ℵ (read 'aleph'), used without subscript, can refer to the infinite members of the series of cardinal numbers generally. Used with a subscript $\alpha$ (an ordinal number), $\aleph_\alpha$ indicates the $\alpha$th cardinal number in the series of all cardinals. Examples: $\aleph_0$ ('aleph-nought' or 'aleph-null') is the least infinite cardinal, that of the set of natural numbers; $\aleph_1$ is the next larger cardinal; and so on.

*See* Cardinality; Continuum hypothesis; Ordinal (number).

**Algorithm** Basic concept in mathematics and, especially, computability theory. Also called 'effective procedures'. Generally, an algorithm is a calculatory procedure given by a finite set of instructions for computing solutions to a class of mathematical problems. In computability theory, algorithms are finitary rules for computing functions, to be executed mechanically on relevant inputs. In this sense, algorithmic calculation cannot rely upon any special mathematical insight (for example, constructing proofs for unsolved mathematical problems) or upon the outcomes of random processes (for example, rolls of a die). Example: the rules, learned in primary school, for finding sums of columns of figures represent an algorithm, in either sense, for number addition.

*See* Computable function; Decision procedure.

**Algorithmic function** *See* Computable function.

**Alternative denial** Term of logic. Refers to a logical operation on propositions that is of the type of the English operator 'It is not the case that both ___ and ___'. In symbolic systems it is commonly represented by '|', the 'Sheffer stroke'. Compounds formed from such operators are true just in case not both of their component sentences are true (that is, just in case at least one of their component sentences is false). Alternative denial is one of two single propositional operators that is, by itself, a complete set of connectives.

*See* Complete set of connectives.

**Ambiguity, fallacy of** Term of logic; an informal fallacy or class of informal fallacies. One commits a fallacy of ambiguity when the crux of one's argument turns on the use of a single word or expression in two distinct meanings or senses. A common fallacy falling under this category is that of equivocation, in which an argument depends crucially upon the use of an ambiguous word in two different senses. Example: 'Gerry is good and she is a violinist; therefore, she is a good violinist'.

**Ampliation** Term of traditional logic. Signifies an argument or inference in which the conclusion 'goes beyond' the premises in the sense that the joint truth of the latter does not guarantee the truth of the former. It is thus a generalization of the traditional conception of inductive inference characterized as reasoning from particular to general.

**Analytic/synthetic (judgment or proposition)** Notions of modern logic. In more recent philosophy the term 'analytic' is generally applied to propositions that are true by dint of their forms or the meanings of their constituent terms. A judgment or proposition of subject–predicate form is analytic if the predicate (concept) is 'contained in' the subject (concept). Kant's way of putting this was to say that in an analytic judgment the predicate is *thought* in (the very act of) *thinking* the subject. Analytic judgments are opposed to *synthetic* judgments, which are defined as judgments in which thinking the subject does not entail thinking the predicate (though the two may legitimately be associated by other means).

**Ancestral (of a relation)** Term of set theory. Also called 'transitive closure'. When $R$ is a binary relation on a set $A$, the ancestral of $R$ (relative to $A$) is the set of ordered pairs $\langle a, b \rangle$ of elements of $A$ such that $a$ and $b$ are $R$-related via a finite chain of elements of $A$. Put more formally, the ancestral is the set of ordered pairs $\langle a, b \rangle$ such that either $Rab$ or there exists a chain of elements $x_1, x_2, \ldots, x_n$ ($n \geqslant 1$) of $A$ such that $Rax_1$, $Rx_ix_{i+1}$ for $1 \leqslant i < n$, and $Rx_nb$.

**Antecedent** Term of logic. The antecedent is the 'if' clause of a conditional of the form 'If... then...'.

*See* Conditional, material.

**Antilogism** In traditional logic, an antilogism or inconsistent triad is a triple of categorical statements so chosen that the joint truth of any two implies the falsity of the third. Christine Ladd-Franklin (1847–1930) proposed antilogism as a test for the validity of a categorical syllogism: a syllogism is valid whenever the triple formed of the two premises and the denial of its conclusion makes an antilogism.

*See* Syllogism, categorical.

**Antisymmetric relation/order** *See* Relations (properties of).

**Apparent variable** *See* Variable.

**Argument** Basic notion of logic. The simplest argument is a set of propositions divided into two: (1) a set of propositions referred to collectively as the *premises*; and (2) a single proposition referred to as the *conclusion*. Complex arguments are built up by suitably arranging a number of simple arguments or steps. The premises, taken together, are supposed to provide a reason for believing the conclusion in the following sense: their joint truth is supposed either to guarantee (in the case of deductive, non-ampliative or demonstrative arguments) or to support to some lesser extent (in the case of inductive, ampliative or non-demonstrative arguments) the truth of the conclusion.

*See* Ampliation; Converse (of an argument); Demonstration; Derivation; Diagonal argument; Dialectical argument; Dilemma; Enthymeme; Fallacy; Immediate inference; Inference; Paradox, *sorites*; Polysyllogism; Proposition; Sophism; Soundness (of an argument); Syllogism, categorical; Syllogism, disjunctive; Syllogism, hypothetical; Syllogism, modal; Validity.

**Argument *ad hominem*** Term of informal logic. Legitimate rhetorical technique by which an arguer persuades an opponent to accept a conclusion by deriving it from premises which the opponent accepts even though the arguer does not. Also often used for the (informal) fallacy of attempting to impugn an argument by denigrating one's opponent; or by arguing that an opponent's views are false or flawed because there is some form of conflict between their circumstances or character traits and the argument.

**Argument *ad ignorantiam*** Term of traditional logic. It signifies a fallacy that argues from the premise that something is not known to be true (false) to the conclusion that it is false (true).

**Argument, converse of an** *See* Converse (of an argument).

**Argument, diagonal** *See* Diagonal argument.

**Argument, dialectical** *See* Dialectical argument.

**Argument (of a relation/function)** *See* Function; Relation.

**Arity** Term of logic and mathematics generally. The arity (or degree or adicity) of a *relation* is the maximum number of items to which the relation properly applies at one time. The arity of a *function* is the number of inputs required to evaluate the function. Note that when a function $y = f(x_1, \ldots, x_n)$ is treated as a relation $Rx_1 \ldots x_n y$, the relation has arity one greater than that of the original function. Examples: the 'less than' relation of arithmetic has arity two; it is a binary relation. The squaring function on the integers has arity one and is called a unary relation.

**Asymmetric relation/order** *See* Relations (properties of).

**Atomic (sentence or formula)** Notion of logic. Within a formal language, a sentence or formula is atomic when the formation rules of the language do not analyse it as compounded from other sentences or formulas of the language. Such a formula or sentence is also called a 'base component'. Occasionally, negations of atomic sentences are also included among the atomic sentences.

**Automaton** Basic notion in computability and formal language theory. An automaton is a finitistic, abstract machine or idealized computing device whose input-output behaviour is used to classify formal languages, sets and mathematical functions according to their computational tractability. Examples: Turing machines are automata and the sets of numbers accepted by Turing machines are precisely the recursively enumerable sets.

*See* Recursively enumerable set; Turing machine.

**Automorphism** Term of model theory and algebra. Signifies an isomorphism whose domain and range are the same set.

*See* Isomorphism.

**Axiom** Term of traditional and modern logic. An axiom is a proposition of a theory that is treated as fundamental or not admitting of proof. Traditionally, axioms were also treated as epistemically basic in various senses (for example, as being self-evident or as not requiring proof for their acceptance). In modern axiomatic systems, *logical* axioms are the propositions that are fundamental in presenting the underlying logic of the theory (for example, the law of the excluded middle), and *proper* axioms are the propositions that are fundamental in presenting the non-logical or substantive truths of the theory (for example, in usual axiomatizations of the arithmetic of the natural numbers, the law that 0 has no predecessor).

**Axiom of abstraction** *See* Axiom of comprehension.

**Axiom of choice** Controversial principle of set theory used implicitly in the nineteenth century and formulated explicitly by Zermelo in 1904 for use in his proof of the well-ordering theorem. Also known as the multiplicative axiom. There are different versions of the axiom of choice in modern set theory. In its most familiar statement, it is understood to guarantee, for every set $A$ of non-empty sets $x$, a choice set, which is a set containing exactly one member from each $x$ in $A$. It is essential to proofs of standard mathematical results concerning the transfinite. It is also equivalent to other noteworthy principles, among them Zorn's lemma. Thanks to celebrated theorems of Gödel and of Paul Cohen, we know that it is neither refutable nor provable from standard axioms for sets, such as those of Zermelo–Fraenkel set theory, provided that they are consistent.

*See* Choice set/function; Zermelo–Fraenkel set theory; Zorn's lemma.

**Axiom of comprehension** Existence principle in set or class theory. Also known as the axiom of abstraction. It was based on Cantor's conception of a set as any 'comprehension' into a whole of distinct objects of our intuition or thought. This suggests that every concept should give rise to a set containing all and only those objects falling under it. A more mind-independent formulation of the axiom was soon proposed which said that every property gives rise to a set containing all and only those objects that have the property. The unrestricted (also sometimes called the 'naïve') version of the principle states that, whenever $P$ is a property, there is a collection $\{x: P(x)\}$ containing precisely those items that have $P$. Frege included a version of this principle in his *Grundgesetze* system for the foundations of mathematics. Famously, this was shown to be inconsistent by Russell in 1902 in what has come to be known as Russell's paradox, by letting $P$ be the property of non-self-membership.

*See* Axiom of reducibility; Class; Paradox, Russell's; Von Neumann–Bernays–Gödel set theory.

**Axiom of constructibility** Nonstandard principle of set theory first propounded by Gödel in 1938. A set is constructible (or belongs to the universe $L$ of constructible sets) when it can be defined from the ordinal numbers using definition schemes whose quantifiers are restricted. Gödel's axiom of constructibility (or $\mathbf{V} = L$) asserts that every set is constructible. Gödel proved that the axiom of choice and the continuum hypothesis are consistent with standard set theory by showing them derivable from $\mathbf{V} = L$. The axiom of constructibility is neither provable nor refutable from standard set-theoretic axioms, if they are consistent. Although $\mathbf{V} = L$ continues to play a crucial role in the investigation of set theory, most contemporary set theorists would not treat it as expressing a truth about sets.

**Axiom of determinateness** *See* Axiom of extensionality.

**Axiom of extensionality** Basic axiom of set theory used in Zermelo's 1908 axiomatization of set theory. Also known as the axiom of determinateness. It states that two sets are identical if and only if they have exactly the same elements. Sometimes, the axiom is interpreted as elucidating our concept of a set as a collection exhausted by its members. Viewed in this way, it gives a basic difference between the concept of a set and the concept of a property.

*See* Von Neumann–Bernays–Gödel set theory; Zermelo–Fraenkel set theory.

**Axiom of foundation** Principle of set theory first formulated as an axiom in 1925 by John von Neumann (although mentioned earlier by Mirimanoff (1917) and by Skolem (1923); and named by Zermelo in 1930). Sometimes also called the axiom of regularity or the axiom of restriction. It states that every non-empty set $A$ has a member $a$ such that $A$ and $a$ have no elements in common ($A \cap a = \emptyset$). In the usual set theories, foundation implies that no set can be a member of itself and that infinitely-descending membership chains cannot occur. It also arranges sets into a hierarchy (called the iterative hierarchy) and allows one to define sets by induction on the membership relation.

*See* Von Neumann–Bernays–Gödel set theory; Zermelo–Fraenkel set theory.

**Axiom of infinity** Principle of set or type theory, variously formulated, requiring the existence of an infinite number of objects of the theory. In the type theory of *Principia Mathematica* (1910), Whitehead and Russell introduced an axiom of infinity to guarantee infinitely many individuals; items of lowest type. In set theories, axioms of infinity assert the existence of infinite collections. Zermelo included one formulation among his 1908 axioms for Cantor's set theory.

In Zermelo's version the axiom states that there is a set $Z$ of which $\emptyset$ (the empty set) is an element and which contains, for each of its elements $e$, the further element $\{e\}$.

*See* Von Neumann–Bernays–Gödel set theory; Zermelo–Fraenkel set theory.

**Axiom of pairing** Axiom of set theory. For any two items $u$ and $v$ there exists a set $w = \{u, v\}$.

*See* Von Neumann–Bernays–Gödel set theory; Zermelo–Fraenkel set theory.

**Axiom of power set** Principle of set theory included by Zermelo in his 1908 axioms for set theory. It states that for every set $A$, there is a further set $\wp(A)$, the power set of $A$, whose elements are exactly the subsets of $A$.

*See* Cantor's theorem; Von Neumann–Bernays–Gödel set theory; Zermelo–Fraenkel set theory.

**Axiom of reducibility** Axiom proposed by Russell as a weakened form of the axiom of comprehension and included in the ramified type theory of Whitehead and Russell's *Principia Mathematica* (1910). Let a predicative function be a propositional function in which no quantifiers occur. It states that, for every propositional function of any order, there is a predicative function. The axiom was used to formalize certain mathematical inductions within their type theory.

**Axiom of regularity** *See* Axiom of foundation.

**Axiom of replacement** Axiom schema of set theory first formulated by Dmitry Mirimanoff in 1917; rediscovered by Fraenkel (1922) and Skolem (1923). Also known as the axiom of substitution. It guarantees that whenever a collection of inputs $x$ to a function $f$ comprises a set, so does the collection of correlative outputs $f(x)$. Among other things, replacement allows one to conclude that unions of countable sequences of sets exist.

*See* Von Neumann–Bernays–Gödel set theory; Zermelo–Fraenkel set theory.

**Axiom of restriction** *See* Axiom of foundation.

**Axiom of separation** Principle of set theory included by Zermelo in his 1908 axioms for set theory; later reformulated by Skolem. It permits one to separate off those elements of a given set which satisfy a given property. Stated more formally, it says that whenever $A$ is a set and $P$ is a well-defined property of $A$, the collection of precisely those members of $A$ possessing $P$ is also a set.

*See* Zermelo–Fraenkel set theory.

**Axiom of substitution** *See* Axiom of replacement.

**Axiom of sumset** *See* Axiom of union.

**Axiom of union** Axiom of Zermelo's 1908 axiomatization of set theory. Also known as the sumset axiom. It states that for any set $A$, there exists a further set $\cup A$ whose elements are exactly the elements of the elements of $A$.

*See* Von Neumann–Bernays–Gödel set theory; Zermelo–Fraenkel set theory.

**Axiom schema** Term of modern logic. An axiom schema is an expression which employs schematic 'letters' (metalinguistic variables) and which determines an infinity of particular axioms, one for each substitution of a definite expression of the appropriate sort for the schematic letters. A classic example is the axiom schema of induction in first-order arithmetic. It is formulated as

$$(\phi(0) \,\&\, \forall x(\phi x \rightarrow \phi x')) \rightarrow \forall x \phi x,$$

where $\phi$ is schematic for well-formed formulas of the language. When such an expression is substituted for $\phi$, we get an axiom of first-order arithmetic.

**Axiomatic theory** Basic concept of modern logic. A theory is said to be *axiomatized* by a set of sentences $A$ (its axioms) when it is the deductive closure of $A$. It is said to be *axiomatizable* just in case it is the deductive closure of some subset of its axioms. It is said to be *recursively axiomatizable* just in case it is the deductive closure of some recursive subset of its axioms. It is said to be *finitely axiomatizable* just in case it is the deductive closure of some finite subset of its axioms.

*See* Closure (deductive/logical); Recursive set.

**Axioms, set-theoretic** The fundamental principles of one or another systematization of set theory.

*See* Von Neumann–Bernays–Gödel set theory; Zermelo–Fraenkel set theory.

# B

**Bamalip** *See* Mood (of a categorical syllogism).

**Bamana** *See* Mood (of a categorical syllogism).

**Baralipton** *See* Mood (of a categorical syllogism).

**Barbara** *See* Mood (of a categorical syllogism).

**Barbari** *See* Mood (of a categorical syllogism).

**Baroco** *See* Mood (of a categorical syllogism).

**Base component** *See* Atomic (sentence or formula).

**Base (of propositional operators/connectives)** *See* Complete set of connectives.

**Begging the question** *See* Circular reasoning, fallacy of.

**Bernays–Gödel set theory** *See* Von Neumann–Bernays–Gödel set theory.

**Berry's paradox** *See* Paradox, Berry's.

**Beths** Set-theoretic notation for the sequence of infinite cardinal numbers generated from the cardinality of the set of natural numbers by applying the power set operation. The first beth number, $\beth_0$, is, accordingly, the cardinal of the set of natural numbers ($\beth_0 = \aleph_0$); each succeeding beth number is the cardinality of the set of all subsets – the power set – of the preceding one. So $\beth_{\alpha+1} = 2^{\beth_\alpha}$ for all ordinals $\alpha$. The continuum hypothesis amounts to the claim that $\aleph_1 = \beth_1$.

*See* Alephs; Cardinality; Continuum hypothesis.

**Biconditional** Term of propositional logic. A biconditional is an operator for joining two sentences that is true just in case its component sentences have the same truth-value (both true or both false); also the compound sentence so formed. The typical example in English is the operator 'if and only if' (often written 'iff').

**Bijection** Term of set theory and mathematics generally. A function is said to be a bijection when it is both *one-one* and *onto* (in other words, when it is both an injection and a surjection). If $f : A \to B$ is a bijection then for any $b$ in $B$ there is exactly one $a$ in $A$ such that $f(a) = b$.

**Bivalence** Semantic principle and characteristic of certain sorts of formal semantics. As an informal semantic principle, bivalence asserts that any unambiguous statement is determinately either true or false. In formal logic, a semantics is bivalent when it assigns, to each well-formed sentence, one or the other of two truth-values. Bivalence, in either sense, ought to be distinguished sharply from the law of excluded middle.

*See* Law of (the) excluded middle.

**Bocardo** *See* Mood (of a categorical syllogism).

**Bound (occurrence of a) variable** *See* Variable.

**Bound (of a set)** Term of set theory and mathematics generally. Refers to a property of ordered sets. An element $a$ is an *upper* bound of a set $A$ if $a$ is greater than or equal to every element of $A$; $a$ is a *least* upper bound (lub or *supremum*) of $A$ if $a$ is an upper bound of $A$ that is less than or equal to all upper bounds of $A$. More formally, if the set $A$ is ordered by the relation $R$, then $a$ is an upper bound of $A$ if $Rxa$ for all $x$ in $A$; and $a$ is a least upper bound if, in addition, $Ray$ for all upper bounds $y$ of $A$. The concepts of *lower* bound and greatest lower bound (glb or *infimum*) are defined analogously.

**Bramantip** *See* Mood (of a categorical syllogism).

**Brouwer's continuity theorem** *See* Choice sequence.

**Burali-Forti's paradox** *See* Paradox, Burali-Forti's.

# C

**Calculus** *See* Formal system.

**Calemes** *See* Mood (of a categorical syllogism).

**Calemop** *See* Mood (of a categorical syllogism).

**Calemos** *See* Mood (of a categorical syllogism).

**Camene** *See* Mood (of a categorical syllogism).

**Camenes** *See* Mood (of a categorical syllogism).

**Camenop** *See* Mood (of a categorical syllogism).

**Camestres** *See* Mood (of a categorical syllogism).

**Camestrop** *See* Mood (of a categorical syllogism).

**Cantor's paradox** *See* Paradox, Cantor's.

**Cantor's theorem** Basic result in set theory, proved by Cantor in 1892. It states that the power set $\wp(A)$ of a set $A$ is always of greater size or cardinality than $A$. Indeed, if $A$ has cardinality $\alpha$, then $\wp(A)$ has cardinality $2^{\alpha}$.

*See* Axiom of power set; Cardinality; Power set.

**Cardinal (number)** *See* Cardinality; Large cardinal.

**Cardinality** Concept of set theory. Two sets $A$ and $B$ have the same cardinality (or power) if and only if there is a bijection from $A$ to $B$. When sets are of the same cardinality they are often treated as having the same size. Cardinal numbers measure cardinality. Hence, two sets have the same cardinal number just in case they have the same cardinality.

Example: Cantor showed that the sets of natural numbers and integers have the same cardinal number, $\aleph_0$ ('aleph-nought').

*See* Alephs; Beths; Equinumerosity/equipollence; Large cardinal; Transfinite cardinal.

**Cartesian product** Term of set theory. Also called the 'cross product' or 'direct product'. The Cartesian product $A_1 \times \ldots \times A_n$ of a family of sets $A_1, \ldots, A_n$ is the class of those ordered $n$-tuples $\langle a_1, \ldots, a_n \rangle$ such that $a_i \in A_i$ for $1 \leqslant i \leqslant n$.

**Categoremata** Term of traditional logic. Signifies a term which can serve as a subject or predicate of a categorical proposition. Contrasted with syncategoremata. Examples: 'horse', 'red', 'Greek'.

*See* Syncategoremata.

**Categorical in power** $\kappa$ Important model-theoretic property of formal theories. When $\kappa$ is a cardinal number, a theory is categorical in power $\kappa$ whenever it has a model whose domain has cardinality $\kappa$ and all of its models with domains of that cardinality are isomorphic. Equivalently, a theory is categorical in power $\kappa$ if it has, up to isomorphism, a unique model of cardinality $\kappa$. Example: the theory of dense, total orders without endpoints is categorical in power $\aleph_0$.

*See* Cardinality; Structure.

**Categorical proposition** Basic notion of traditional logic. A categorical proposition is a subject–predicate sentence consisting of a quantifier, two terms (the *minor* or *subject* term and the *major* or *predicate* term) and a copula (negated or not). (The name comes from the Greek '*katēgoreīn*', 'to predicate'.) Two possible quantifiers and two copulas yield four categorical forms, universal ('all', 'every') or particular ('some') in quantity, affirmative ('are') or negative ('are not') in quality (sign of the copula). In the Middle Ages these came to be called by the first four vowels:

*A* All *A* are *B* (universal affirmative);
*E* No *A* are *B* (universal negative);
*I* Some *A* are *B* (particular affirmative);
*O* Some *A* are not *B* (particular negative).

In *De interpretatione* Aristotle recognizes also 'indefinite' categorical propositions, which lack a quantifier. Their precise interpretation remains a matter of dispute.

*See* Mood (of a categorical syllogism); Opposition; Syllogism, categorical.

**Categorical syllogism** *See* Syllogism, categorical.

**Categorical theory** Important model-theoretic property of formal theories. A theory is categorical (or has the categoricity property) whenever it has a model and all of its models are isomorphic. Equivalently, a theory is categorical if it has, up to isomorphism, a unique model. Example: second-order Peano arithmetic is categorical.

*See* Structure.

**Celantes** *See* Mood (of a categorical syllogism).

**Celantop** *See* Mood (of a categorical syllogism).

**Celantos** *See* Mood (of a categorical syllogism).

**Celarent** *See* Mood (of a categorical syllogism).

**Celaro** *See* Mood (of a categorical syllogism).

**Celaront** *See* Mood (of a categorical syllogism).

**Cesare** *See* Mood (of a categorical syllogism).

**Cesaro** *See* Mood (of a categorical syllogism).

**Characteristic function** Term of set theory and mathematics generally. The characteristic function of a set is the function which maps the members of the set to 1 and all other elements to 0.

$$\chi_A(x) = \begin{cases} 1 & \text{if } x \in A \\ 0 & \text{if } x \notin A \end{cases}$$

*See* Recursive set; Recursively enumerable set.

**Choice, axiom of** *See* Axiom of choice.

**Choice sequence** Concept introduced into the intuitionistic theory of real numbers by Brouwer (inspired by ideas of du Bois-Reymond and Borel) around 1914. In intuitionistic mathematics, a choice sequence is a mapping from the natural numbers into a collection (usually the natural numbers or the rational numbers) and is considered an 'incomplete entity' in that values which the sequence will attain may not be conceived as fully determined in advance by either logic, explicit rule or stipulation. Brouwer discovered proofs of his famous continuity theorem – that all total real-valued functions over the unit interval are uniformly continuous – from reflection upon his conception of choice sequence.

**Choice set/function** Sets or functions, respectively, which are guaranteed to exist by the axiom of choice. Let $A$ be a collection of non-empty sets $x$. A choice *set* for $A$ is a set containing precisely one element from each $x$. A choice *function* for $A$ is a function which takes each $x$ in $A$ to an element of itself: for each $x$ in $A$, $f(x) \in x$.

*See* Axiom of choice.

**Church's theorem** A major result in the metamathematics of first-order logic, proved by Church in 1936. Church's theorem asserts that validity in full first-order logic is undecidable; equivalently, that there is no decision procedure for determining whether or not an arbitrary formula in full first-order predicate logic is a theorem. In fact, it is possible to show that validity is undecidable for any first-order language containing at least one binary predicate symbol. Church's theorem yields a definitive negative solution to Hilbert's *Entscheidungsproblem* (decision problem) for elementary logic.

*See* Decidability; Decision procedure; Solvable problem; Validity.

**Church's thesis** A claim which is foundational for abstract computability and recursion theory, first put forward by Church. Also known as the Church–Turing thesis. Church's thesis maintains that a mathematical function is computable mechanically by intuitive algorithm just in case it is Turing computable or, equivalently, is recursive. Church's thesis is widely thought not to admit of definitive proof, although certain forms of evidence for it can be adduced.

*See* Algorithm; Recursive function; Turing computable function.

**Church–Turing thesis** *See* Church's thesis.

**Circular reasoning, fallacy of** Term of logic; an informal fallacy or class of informal fallacies, also known as arguing in a circle, begging the question and *petitio principii*. An argument exhibits circular reasoning when, explicitly or implicitly, it assumes its conclusion, or a claim tantamount to the conclusion, among its premises. To accept the premises of a circular argument, one must already have accepted its conclusion.

**Class** Basic concept of set and class theory. Generally, a class is the extension of a property. Certain abstract set theories – for example, von Neumann–Bernays–Gödel – distinguish between sets and classes, taking classes to be arbitrary collections of sets, some of which may well be sets themselves. Those classes which are not sets, such as the class of all sets and the class of all ordinals, are called *proper* classes.

*See* Axiom of comprehension; Paradox, Burali-Forti's; Von Neumann–Bernays–Gödel set theory.

**Class/set distinction** *See* Von Neumann–Bernays–Gödel set theory.

**Closed term/formula** Notion of predicate logic. Signifies a term or formula that contains no free occurrence of a bindable variable.

*See* Variable.

**Closure (deductive, logical)** Term of metalogic. A set *A* of sentences of a language *L* is deductively closed just in case every sentence of *L* that is deducible from *A* is an element of *A*. The deductive closure of a set *A* is the set of all sentences deducible from *A*. *Deductive* closure is a syntactic notion. *Logical* closure is a semantic notion which obtains when a set *A* of sentences of *L* contains every sentence of *L* that follows validly from *A*.

**Codomain** *See* Range (of a relation/function).

**Compact cardinal** *See* Large cardinal.

**Compactness** Semantic property of formal systems in modern logic and a leading idea in model theory. A formal system is compact just in case the semantic consistency or satisfiability of every set of formulas is finitely determined; that is, a set is satisfiable whenever all its finite subsets are. Equivalently, a system is compact if whenever a sentence *S* is a logical consequence of a set of sentences Γ, *S* is a logical consequence of some finite subset of Γ. Classical propositional logic and first-order logic are both compact (as proved by Gödel and Maltsev), the latter fact being of crucial importance in the model theory of first-order languages. Classical second-order logic, however, is not compact.

*See* Consistency; Satisfaction.

**Comparability** *See* Law of trichotomy.

**Complement** Term of set theory and mathematics generally. Generally speaking, the complement of a *class* is the collection of things not in it. In set theory, this definition is most often too general and leads to contradiction. It is therefore replaced by the notion of a *relative* complement (that is, a complement relativized to a given set, which may be the universe of discourse). $C(B)$ is the complement of the *set* $B$ relative to a given set $A$ just in case $C(B)$ comprises all elements in $A$ that are not in $B$. The complement relative to a set $A$ of an $n$-ary *relation* $R$ is the set of all $n$-tuples $\langle a_1, \ldots, a_n \rangle$ such that not-$Ra_1 \ldots a_n$.

**Complete relation/order** *See* Relations (properties of).

**Complete set of connectives** A term from the metatheory of formal propositional logic. A set of propositional connectives is complete – or expressively complete (or functionally complete or a *base*) – just in case every truth-function is expressed by some propositional formula employing only connectives from the set. Examples: the sets $\{\neg, \vee, \&\}$, $\{\neg, \vee\}$, $\{\neg, \&\}$ and $\{\neg, \rightarrow\}$ are all complete. The set $\{\neg, \leftrightarrow\}$ is not. The only single binary connectives that are complete by themselves are Sheffer's alternative denial (the 'Sheffer stroke', written '$p \mid q$' and read 'not both $p$ and $q$'), and Peirce's joint denial (written '$p \downarrow q$' and read 'not $p$ and not $q$').

**Completeness (of a logical calculus)** Term of metalogic. A logical calculus is *weakly* complete if every logical truth is a logical theorem; in other words, if it proves every logically valid sentence of its language. If one is interested in formalizing the more general notion of logical consequence, then one will require that the calculus is also *strongly* complete, that is, whenever a sentence $S$ is a logical consequence of a set of premises $\Gamma$, there is a derivation of $S$ from $\Gamma$; in other words, every sentence validly implied by the axioms is provable.

*See* Completeness theorem; Soundness (of a logical calculus).

**Completeness (of a theory)** Term of metamathematics. A theory is said to be complete when all valid sentences of the language of the theory are theorems of the theory. If classical truth is the notion of truth assumed, a theory is complete (sometimes 'negation-complete') if for any sentence $S$ of the language of the theory, either $S$ or not-$S$ is a theorem.

Examples: first-order Peano arithmetic is incomplete, but second-order Peano arithmetic is complete.

*See* Theory.

**Completeness theorem** Common name for the theorem first proved by Gödel in 1930 that every consistent set of sentences of a first-order calculus or quantificational language has a model. From this it follows that the calculus is both weakly and strongly complete.

*See* Completeness (of a logical calculus).

**Composition, fallacy of** Term of logic; an informal fallacy. One commits the fallacy of composition by inferring illicitly, from the premise that parts or members of a thing share a certain property, that the whole thing also has the property. The fallacy of composition is converse to that of division. Example: 'Each being in nature serves a discernible purpose; therefore, nature itself serves a discernible purpose'.

**Comprehension** *See* Abstraction; Axiom of comprehension; Intension.

**Computable function** Essential notion in abstract computability theory. A mathematical function $f$ is computable whenever there is an algorithm or finitary mechanical procedure which will accept any $x$ for which $f$ is defined and, after a finite series of steps, produce the appropriate value $f(x)$ of the function at $x$. Computable functions are also called 'effectively computable', 'effectively calculable' or 'algorithmic' functions. Since the early 1930s, a variety of mathematically rigorous explications of computable function have been offered, among them Turing computable function and recursive function.

*See* Algorithm; Recursive function; Turing computable function.

**Conclusion** *See* Argument.

**Conditional, counterfactual** Term of philosophical logic. Also known as 'contrary to fact conditionals' or 'subjunctive conditionals', these are any of a variety of conditional or 'If... then...' statements in which the antecedent states a condition which the speaker assumes to be unsatisfied. Example: 'If Oswald hadn't killed Kennedy, someone else would have'. (Contrast 'If Oswald didn't kill Kennedy, someone else did'.) Counterfactual conditionals are neither truth-functional nor strict conditionals and the issue of proper logical rules and semantics to govern them continues to spark debate in philosophical logic.

*See* Conditional, material.

**Conditional, material** Term of logic. Sometimes also known as the Philonian conditional. It is a statement which places a condition, called the 'antecedent', on the obtaining of another statement, called the 'consequent'. A material conditional is false when the antecedent is true and the consequent false. Otherwise, it is true. 'If..., then ___', '___ if...' and '...only if ___' are expressions in English that are often used to express material conditionals. In each of these, the antecedent is the sentence that goes in the place of '...', and the consequent the sentence that goes in the place of '___'.

*See* Conditional, counterfactual; Paradoxes of material and strict implication.

**Conditional proof** Term of logic and mathematics. Signifies a type of proof in which one deduces a conclusion $C$ from a list of assumed premises $P_1, \ldots, P_n$ and asserts on the basis of this the conditional proposition 'If $P_1$ and $P_2$ and... and $P_n$, then $C$'.

**Conjunction** Term of propositional logic. Refers to operators (generally binary) for forming compound sentences that are true just in case all of their component sentences are true. Also refers to the compound sentences formed in this way. The typical example in English is the operator 'and'.

**Conjunctive normal form** *See* Normal form (conjunctive).

**Connected relation/order** *See* Relations (properties of).

**Connective** *See* Propositional operator/connective.

**Connotation** Used generally for the ideas or intellectual and emotive associations brought forth by a word, in contrast to its denotation. John Stuart Mill employed the contrast denotation/connotation as a semantics for common nouns in his *System of Logic* (1843). For Mill, the connotation of a common noun is the set of general characteristics commonly associated with it, characteristics which Mill believed to determine the range of items to which the term properly applies. Example: the descriptions 'the male human lead of *Every Which Way But Loose*' and 'the mayor of Carmel, California' at one time had the same denotation but have different connotations.

*See* Denotation; Extension; Intension.

**Consequent** Term of logic. The consequent is the 'then' clause of a conditional of the form 'If... then...'.

*See* Affirming the consequent, fallacy of; Conditional, material.

**Consequentiae** Valid forms of conditionals or of logical consequence in the logic of Boethius and others. While the conditional form was used, it is a matter of interpretation whether logical consequence was not in fact intended.

**Conservative extension (of a theory)** *See* Extension (of a theory).

**Consistency** Basic notion of metalogic. In the *syntactic* sense, a set $\Gamma$ of sentences or propositions is said to be consistent (satisfiable) just in case there is no sentence $S$ such that both $S$ and $\neg S$ are derivable from $\Gamma$. In the *semantic* sense, $\Gamma$ is consistent just in case there is no proposition $S$ such that both $S$ and $\neg S$ are logically implied by $\Gamma$.

*See* Satisfaction.

**Constant** In mathematics and science generally, a quantity or linguistic expression having, in the context, a fixed, determinate value, such as $\pi$, the speed of light or the gravitational constant. In logic, constants represent, syntactically, those places and patterns in a formal expression not open to government by a quantifier or other binding operator. Semantically, constants are those elements of an expression which do not range over various values after an interpretation of the language has been fixed. *Logical* constants are those formal items which never permit re-interpretation; standardly, these include connectives and quantifiers. Predicate and individual constants are those which, under a given interpretation, are assigned fixed subsets of or elements from the domain of interpretation.

**Constant function** A constant function takes every input to the same constant output value: for all $x$, $f_a(x) = a$.

*See* Function; Recursive function.

**Constructibility, axiom of** *See* Axiom of constructibility.

**Constructive choices, principle of** *See* Markov's principle.

**Constructive existence proof** A constructive existence proof is any mathematical proof or derivation in a formal system of an existential conclusion 'There is something that is *A*' in which a means is provided for properly describing, producing or constructing a suitable item which is provably an *A*. This style of proof, favoured by mathematical intuitionists and constructivists, contrasts with nonconstructive existence proofs, in which existential conclusions are deduced by such alternative means as reducing to absurdity the supposition that everything fails to be *A*.

**Continuity theorem** *See* Choice sequence.

**Continuous set** Term of set theory and mathematics generally. A set ordered by a dense ordering is continuous when each of its subsets which is bounded above has a least upper bound and each of its subsets which is bounded below has a greatest lower bound. In a continuous set no element has a predecessor or a successor. Contrast with a discrete set.

*See* Bound (of a set); Discrete set; Ordering; Predecessor; Relations (properties of); Successor.

**Continuum hypothesis** Problem of set theory first raised by Cantor in 1878. The smallest infinite class is that of the natural numbers $0, 1, 2, \ldots$, whose size is denoted by $\aleph_0$. The continuum (the class of real numbers) is isomorphic to the power set of the natural numbers so, by Cantor's theorem, the continuum is larger than the class of natural numbers. The continuum *problem* is the problem of determining whether the continuum is the very next largest size (cardinality) of infinite class after that of the natural numbers or whether there are infinite classes of intermediate size. Cantor conjectured that there are not. This conjecture has come to be known as the continuum hypothesis (in symbols, $\aleph_1 = 2^{\aleph_0}$). The *generalized* continuum hypothesis is the conjecture that this same structure holds for the entire increasing series of infinite class sizes: that is, for every size of infinite class $\aleph_\alpha$, one obtains the next largest cardinal $\aleph_{\alpha+1}$ by forming the power set of a set of cardinality $\aleph_\alpha$. David Hilbert, in his famous address of 1900, put the construction of a proof of the continuum hypothesis on his list of foremost outstanding mathematical problems. In 1938, Gödel proved the generalized continuum hypothesis to be consistent with axioms of set theory; and in 1963, Paul Cohen proved it independent of those axioms.

*See* Alephs; Beths; Cantor's theorem.

**Contraction** Term of modern logic. A type of structural rule in sequent systems. Roughly it signifies a modification of a valid argument or inference in which repetition of premises is eliminated or diminished.

**Contradiction** Basic notion of logic. A proposition is said to be a contradiction when it is logically impossible that it be true or, equivalently, when it is logically necessary that it be false. Example: any proposition of the form '*p* and not *p*' is a contradiction.

*See Ex falso quodlibet.*

**Contradiction, law of** *See* Law of contradiction.

**Contradictories** *See* Opposition.

**Contraposition** Basic notion of logic. In *sentential* logic, turning a sentence 'If *p* then *q*' around to 'If not-*q* then not-*p*' (called the contrapositive of the original sentence) is contraposition. This is valid in most logics of conditionals. In *Aristotelian* logic, contraposition refers to the valid immediate inference forms 'All *A* are *B*; therefore all non-*B* are non-*A*' and 'Some *A* are not *B*; therefore some non-*B* are not non-*A*' and their converses.

*See* Immediate inference.

**Contraries** *See* Opposition.

**Contrary to fact conditional** *See* Conditional, counterfactual.

**Converse domain** *See* Range (of a relation/function).

**Converse (of an argument)** Term of logic. The converse of an argument '*P*; therefore *Q*' is the argument '*Q*; therefore *P*', obtained by interchanging the premise and conclusion.

**Converse (of a conditional)** Term of logic. The converse of a conditional 'If *P*, then *Q*' is the conditional 'If *Q*, then *P*', obtained by interchanging the antecedent and consequent.

**Converse (of a relation)** Term of logic and set theory. The converse (or inverse) of a relation $R$ is the relation $\breve{R}$ such that $\breve{R}xy$ if and only if $Ryx$.

**Conversion *per accidens*** Term of traditional logic. This refers to two modes of immediate inference in syllogistic: 'All *A* are *B*; therefore some *B* are *A*'; and 'No *A* are *B*; therefore some *B* are not *A*'. Valid only under the existential assumption that there are *A*s.

*See* Immediate inference.

**Conversion, simple** Term of traditional logic. This refers to two modes valid modes of immediate inference supporting equivalences in syllogistic: 'Some *A* are *B*; therefore some *B* are *A*'; and 'No *A* are *B*; therefore no *B* are *A*'. See Immediate inference.

**Copula** Any form of the verb 'to be' (or its negation) linking subject and predicate. In traditional logic, 'is not/are not' was sometimes called a negative copula.

*See* Categorical proposition.

**Countable** Term of set theory. A set is countable (or denumerable) when it is either empty or can be exhaustively listed using the natural numbers. Equivalently, a set is countable when it is in one-one correspondence with the set of natural numbers. Any set which is not countable is called uncountable.

**Counter domain** *See* Range (of a relation/function).

**Counterfactual (conditional)** *See* Conditional, counterfactual.

**Cross product (of sets)** *See* Cartesian product.

**Curry's paradox** *See* Paradox, Curry's.

**Cut-elimination theorems** A class of crucial results in the proof theory of formal logics, the first theorem of which was stated and proved in 1934 by Gentzen (though anticipated by Herbrand). Gentzen's cut-elimination theorem is also known as the '*Hauptsatz*' (main theorem). When formulated as a sequent calculus (that is, as a system representing logical consequence immediately) first-order predicate logic naturally contains a 'cut rule' for eliminating extra hypotheses. In a simple case, such a rule states 'If *A* derives *B* or *C*, while *A* and *C* derives *D*, then *A* derives *B* or *D*', hence cutting the extra hypothesis *C*. Gentzen showed how to convert every proof in his system into a (possibly much longer) cut-free proof. Cut-elimination theorems have been formulated and proved for a wide variety of formal systems, including arithmetic and predicative analysis, and shed considerable light on issues of provability and consistency.

# D

**Dabitis** *See* Mood (of a categorical syllogism).

**Darapti** *See* Mood (of a categorical syllogism).

**Daraptis** *See* Mood (of a categorical syllogism).

**Darii** *See* Mood (of a categorical syllogism).

**Datisi** *See* Mood (of a categorical syllogism).

***De dicto*** *See De re/de dicto.*

**De Morgan's laws** Theorems of propositional logic and Boolean algebra known, in effect, to medieval logicians but named for De Morgan (1806–71), who stated them as laws for class operations. In propositional logic, De Morgan's laws assert for statements $A$ and $B$

$$\text{not-}(A \text{ and } B) = \text{not-}A \text{ or not-}B$$
$$\text{not-}(A \text{ or } B) = \text{not-}A \text{ and not-}B.$$

***De re/de dicto*** Important distinction in modal and intensional logics. An epistemic or modal expression such as 'possibly' or 'it is known that' is used *de dicto* just in case it is taken as modifying an entire sentence or proposition (dictum). It is used *de re* when it is understood as attributing an epistemic or modal characteristic to some particular item(s) or feature(s) (res) mentioned in the sentence. The distinction, which played an implicit role in Greek logic and an explicit role in medieval logic (Aquinas and Peter of Spain), has received various formulations over the centuries. Modern uses of the distinction tend to focus on singular terms rather than predicates. Quine speaks of a principle of 'exportation' when from a *de dicto* statement such as 'Tom believes that Cicero denounced Catiline', one infers a *de re* statement such as 'Tom believes Cicero to have denounced

Catiline'. Peter of Spain considered such inference fallacious. Examples: when we construe 'It is possible that everyone is married' as putting forward the statement that everyone is married as possibly true, 'it is possible' is used *de dicto*. If we understand 'It is possible that everyone is married' to mean, of each individual person, that they are possibly married, then that possibility is ascribed *de re*.

**Decidability** Basic notion of computability theory and metamathematics. A *set* (for example, of numbers or of formulas in some formal language) is decidable if there is a decision procedure for membership in it, that is, an algorithm which determines for any suitable item (number, formula and so on) whether it is a member of the set. A set is said to be semi-decidable if there is a procedure which reliably confirms when presented with a member of the set that it is a member, but which need not produce an answer at all when presented with a non-member. A *property* is said to be decidable or semi-decidable if the set of items having the property is. A *sentence* $S$ is decidable by or in a theory $T$ just in case either $S$ or $\neg S$ is provable in $T$. Examples: the truth-table method provides a decision procedure for classical propositional logic and shows that the set of propositional tautologies is decidable. The set of valid sentences of predicate logic, on the other hand, is only semi-decidable.

*See* Algorithm; Church's theorem.

**Decision problem** A central notion in metamathematics and computability theory. The decision problem for a set of questions is the problem of giving an algorithm sufficient for correctly answering – positively or negatively – any of the questions in the set. When such an algorithm exists, the decision problem is said to be solvable, otherwise unsolvable. In the case of a formal theory, the decision problem or *Entscheidungsproblem* is one of finding an algorithm which determines, in an arbitrary case, provability in the theory. Examples: the decision problem for evenness of natural numbers is solved by the ordinary 'divide by 2' algorithm. A proof of Church's theorem shows the decision problem for general first-order validity to be unsolvable.

*See* Entscheidungsproblem; Solvable problem.

**Decision procedure** A term of formal logic and computability theory. There is a decision procedure for a general question or problem (such as theoremhood in a formal system) whenever there exists a finitary algorithmic procedure for correctly determining answers to all allowable instances of the question or problem in a uniform fashion. When there is a decision procedure for a problem, the property it determines is said to be decidable. For example, the truth-table method yields a decision procedure for tautology in classical propositional logic and tautologousness is thereby a decidable property of formulas.

*See* Algorithm; Church's theorem.

**Deducibility** Term of metalogic. In a formal system $F$ consisting of a language $L$, axioms and/or rules of inference, a formula $\phi$ of $L$ is said to be deducible from a set of formulas $A$ of $L$ just in case there is a finite sequence of formulas $\phi_1, \ldots, \phi_n$ of $L$ such that $\phi_n$ is $\phi$ and each $\phi_i$, $i < n$, is either an element of $A$, an axiom of $F$ or follows from preceding elements of $\phi_1, \ldots, \phi_n$ by a rule of inference of $F$. In an informal sense, a sentence is said to be deducible from a set of sentences just in case it follows from them by deductive means of reasoning.

*See* Derivation.

**Deduction** *See* Derivation.

**Deduction theorem** A theorem apparently first proved by Tarski in 1921 and first published by Herbrand in 1930. It states that if a formula $B$ can be derived from a set of formulas $\Gamma$ together with a single formula $A$, then the sentence $A \rightarrow B$ can be derived from $\Gamma$. That is, if $\Gamma, A \vdash B$, then $\Gamma \vdash A \rightarrow B$.

**Degree (of a relation)** *See* Arity.

**Demonstration** Term of traditional and modern logic. In modern logic, demonstration is a synonym for 'proof', or deductive reasoning from axiomatic premises. In traditional logic, it is deductive reasoning from premises that are true and fundamental (or necessary); the kinds of premises provided for a student by an ideally informed and organized teacher. In demonstration, a reasoner is taken to proceed from propositions that are fundamental assertions of a subject to a distinct proposition that follows necessarily from them. Contrast with *dialectical* reasoning.

*See* Derivation; Dialectical argument.

**Denial** *See* Alternative denial; Denying the antecedent, fallacy of; Joint denial; Negation.

**Denotation** Term of semantics and formal logic. Within contemporary formal semantics, the denotation of an expression is its semantic value, the entity or entities associated with it under some scheme of interpretation. As conceived by John Stuart Mill in his *System of Logic* (1843), the denotation of a term, in contrast to its connotation, is the collection of items to which the term properly applies. Examples: 'Garrison Keillor' and 'the author of *Lake Wobegon Days*' have the same denotation; the denotation of 'author of *Principia Mathematica*' is the set comprising Bertrand Russell and Alfred North Whitehead.

*See* Connotation; Extension.

**Dense relation/order** *See* Relations (properties of).

**Denumerable** *See* Countable.

**Denying the antecedent, fallacy of** Term of logic; a formal fallacy. The fallacy is committed in arguments which, from a conditional premise ('If *A* then *B*') and the denial of the antecedent of that conditional ('Not *A*'), incorrectly conclude the denial of the consequent ('Not *B*').

**Derivability conditions** Conditions on the arithmetized expressions of provability used in proving such results as (generalized versions of) Gödel's second incompleteness theorem and Löb's theorem. Hilbert and Bernays were the first to provide an explicit statement of such conditions (1939). Their conditions were streamlined by Löb (in 1955 in his solution of Henkin's problem), who simplified them to the following. (The formula $\mathrm{Prov}_T(x)$ 'expresses' the notion of a formula's being provable in $T$ in the limited sense that the set of $A$ such that $\vdash_T \mathrm{Prov}_T(\ulcorner A \urcorner)$ is the set of theorems of $T$. $\ulcorner A \urcorner$ is the numeral in the language of $T$ for the Gödel number of $A$.)

DC1 For all sentences $A$ of the language of a theory $T$, if $A$ is a theorem of $T$, then it is provable in $T$ that $\mathrm{Prov}_T(\ulcorner A \urcorner)$.

DC2 For all sentences $A, B$ of the language of $T$,

$$\text{`}\mathrm{Prov}_T(\ulcorner A \rightarrow B \urcorner) \rightarrow (\mathrm{Prov}_T(\ulcorner A \urcorner) \rightarrow \mathrm{Prov}_T(\ulcorner B \urcorner))\text{'}$$

is a theorem of $T$.

DC3 For every sentence $A$ of the language of $T$,

$$\text{`}\mathrm{Prov}_T(\ulcorner A \urcorner) \rightarrow \mathrm{Prov}_T(\ulcorner \mathrm{Prov}_T(\ulcorner A \urcorner) \urcorner)\text{'}$$

is a theorem of $T$.

*See* Incompleteness theorems; Löb's theorem; Henkin sentence; Henkin's problem; Provability predicate.

**Derivation** Notion of metalogic. A derivation (or deduction) is a syntactic entity which corresponds to an argument, proof or inference in a given formal system of inference or proof. Typically, it is a finite sequence of sentences of a formal language in which the first is an axiom of some sort and each succeeding element is either another axiom or follows from previous elements via the rules of transformation of the system. The conclusion of the derivation is the last element of the sequence. In such a system, a sentence $S$ is said to be derivable if there is a derivation whose last element is $S$.

*See* Constructive existence proof; Deducibility; Demonstration; Formal system; Inference; Proof.

**Determinateness, axiom of** *See* Axiom of extensionality.

**Diagonal argument** A style of proof with many applications in mathematical logic, discovered in the context of real analysis by Paul du Bois-Reymond; later employed in set theory by Cantor and Dedekind. Also referred to as diagonal proof or the diagonalization technique. Cantor used a diagonal argument to prove what is now known as Cantor's theorem. Noteworthy instances of diagonal arguments also include Gödel's first incompleteness theorem and the unsolvability of the halting problem. The term 'diagonal' comes from visualizing diagonal arguments as applying to sets represented as arrays of points infinite in two-dimensions, from which the proof shows how to construct an infinite sequence based upon the diagonal elements in the array. Example: applying the diagonalization technique to the following array can be used to prove that there are countably many (positive) rational numbers.

$$\begin{array}{cccccc}
1 & \frac{1}{2} & \frac{1}{3} & \frac{1}{4} & \frac{1}{5} & \cdots \\
2 & \frac{2}{2} & \frac{2}{3} & \frac{2}{4} & \frac{2}{5} & \cdots \\
3 & \frac{3}{2} & \frac{3}{3} & \frac{3}{4} & \frac{3}{5} & \cdots \\
\vdots & \vdots & \vdots & \vdots & \vdots &
\end{array}$$

*See* Cantor's theorem; Halting problem; Incompleteness theorems.

**Dialectical argument** Term of traditional logic. Historically, it signifies a type of argument that was contrasted with demonstration by the quality of its premises. In a dialectical argument, the premises were not taken to be fundamental, certain, necessary or known; they were not the kinds of premises that an ideally knowledgeable and rational teacher would use to teach a student the conclusion of the argument. Rather, they were adopted only for the sake of argument in order to settle a dispute and represented either generally accepted opinion or, more narrowly still, the opinion of the other side in the dispute.

*See* Demonstration.

**Difference of sets** Term of set theory and mathematics generally. The difference, $A - B$, of two sets $A$ and $B$ is the collection of things that are elements of $A$ but not elements of $B$. The collection of things that are elements of $A$ but not elements of $B$ together with the collection of things that are elements of $B$ but not elements of $A$ is called the *symmetric* difference of $A$ and $B$.

**Dilemma** Term of traditional logic. Also sometimes known as a 'horned syllogism'. It signifies either of two forms of argument in which the first premise or major premise asserts two conditionals. In *constructive* dilemma, the conditionals have different antecedents but the same consequent. The second premise then asserts the disjunction of the antecedents; and the conclusion, the common consequent:

> If *P* then *R*, and if *Q* then *R*.
>
> But either *P* or *Q*.
>
> Therefore *R*.

In *destructive* dilemma, the conditionals have the same antecedent but different consequents. The second premise then asserts the disjunction of the denials of the consequents; and the conclusion, the denial of the common antecedent:

> If *P* then *Q*, and if *P* then *R*.
>
> But either not *Q* or not *R*.
>
> Therefore not *P*.

**Dilution** Term of modern logic. Also called *weakening* or *thinning*. A type of structural rule in sequent systems. Roughly, it refers to any of a variety of modifications of arguments or inferences in which an already valid inference is weakened (diluted) by either conjoining premises to its premises or disjoining conclusions to its conclusion. Sometimes the term is also applied to single arguments where the conclusion is just one of the premises disjoined with another sentence. There the conclusion is referred to as a weakening (dilution) of the premises.

**Dimari** *See* Mood (of a categorical syllogism).

**Dimaris** *See* Mood (of a categorical syllogism).

**Dimatis** *See* Mood (of a categorical syllogism).

**Direct product (of sets)** *See* Cartesian product.

**Direct proof** Term of logic and mathematics. It signifies a type of proof in which one deduces the conclusion directly from the premises of a proof by a series of steps of analysis and/or combination. Contrasted with indirect proof or *reductio ad absurdum*.

**Disamis** *See* Mood (of a categorical syllogism).

**Discourse, domain of** *See* Domain of discourse.

**Discrete set** Term of set theory. An ordered set is discrete if every element (save the largest and the smallest, if there be such) has a predecessor and a successor. Contrast with a continuous set.

*See* Continuous set; Predecessor; Successor.

**Disjunction** Term of propositional logic. Refers to any term that is used to form two sentences into a larger compound sentence where the truth of the compound requires the truth of only one of its component sentences (referred to as its *disjuncts*). The simplest example in English is 'or'. Alternatively, it refers to the compound sentences thus formed. There are two sorts of disjunctions commonly recognized in propositional logic: *inclusive* and *exclusive*. An inclusive disjunctive compound is true just in case at least one of its components is true. An exclusive disjunctive compound is true just in case exactly one of its components is true.

**Disjunctive normal form** *See* Normal form (disjunctive).

**Disjunctive syllogism** *See* Syllogism, disjunctive.

**Distributed term (of a syllogism)** Notion of traditional logic which signifies the way in which a term is used in a categorical proposition. Historically, a distributed term is one that refers to or stands for all members of its extension. One common rule for distribution is that universal (that is, *A* and *E*) propositions distribute their subject terms and *negative* (that is, *E* and *O*) propositions distribute their predicate terms. Another common rule, however, teaches that universal propositions distribute their subjects and that *particular* propositions distribute their predicates. This illustrates the lack of clarity of the central notion of the traditional characterization; namely, that of a term's 'referring to' the elements of its extension.

*See* Categorical proposition.

**Division, fallacy of** Term of logic; an informal fallacy. One commits the fallacy of division by inferring illicitly, from the premise that a whole possesses a certain property, that its parts or members share that property. The fallacy of division is converse to that of composition. Example: 'George is a member of a great football team; therefore, George is a great football player'.

**Domain (of a relation/function)** Term of logic and set theory. Also known as the 'left field' of a relation. The domain of an $n$-ary *relation* $R$ is the collection of $n-1$-tuples $\langle a_1, \ldots, a_{n-1} \rangle$ such that there is an $a_n$ with $Ra_1 \ldots a_n$. The domain of a *function* $f : A \to B$ is the set $A$ on which $f$ is defined.

**Domain of discourse** Term of logic and model theory. Traditionally, it signified the class of things being spoken of in some discourse. In modern logic, it is sometimes the term used for the domain or universe of a structure.

*See* Structure.

**Downward Löwenheim–Skolem theorem** *See* Löwenheim–Skolem theorem(s).

**Duality** Important property of equational laws in Boolean algebra and logical equivalences in classical logic. In Boolean algebra, the duality theorem asserts that an equation expresses a law of Boolean algebra just in case its dual also does. Here, the dual of a Boolean equation results from interchanging the symbol for meet (intersection) with that of join (union), and 0 with 1, throughout the equation. In a language for propositional logic in which disjunction, conjunction and negation are primitives, the dual of a formula is obtained by replacing disjunction by conjunction, and conversely. In this case, whenever two formulas are logically equivalent, so are their duals. The concept was also prominent in early nineteenth-century geometry, where it was noticed that many theorems in plane geometry had duals obtainable by interchanging the term 'line' with the term 'point'.

# E

**Effective procedure** *See* Algorithm.

**Effectively calculable function** *See* Computable function.

**Effectively computable function** *See* Computable function.

**Elementarily equivalent structures** Term of metalogic. Two structures are elementarily equivalent if whenever a first-order sentence is true in one, it is true in the other. Example: first-order arithmetic has nonstandard models which are elementarily equivalent to the intended model.

**Empty set** Concept of set theory. An empty (or null) set is one which contains no members. From the axiom of extensionality, it follows that there is at most one empty set in the universe of sets. Since it has no members, the empty set acts like a zero or identity element for sets under the operations of union and intersection.

**Endomorphism** Term of model theory and algebra. Signifies a homomorphism whose domain and range are the same set. *See* Homomorphism.

**Enthymeme** Term of logic. In modern logic, it signifies any argument which, taken literally, is invalid, but which becomes valid when certain propositions thought too obvious or apparent to require explicit statement are taken as implicit premises. In traditional logic it referred broadly to a syllogism having a missing premise that the reader was supposed to supply.

**Entscheidungsproblem** German for 'decision problem', but usually reserved for one such problem; that of finding a mechanical test for validity in first-order logic. It was shown to be insoluble by Church and Turing independently in 1936.

*See* Church's theorem; Decision problem.

**Epimenides' paradox** *See* Paradox, Epimenides'.

**Equinumerosity/equipollence** Term of set theory. Sets are said to be equipollent, or equinumerous, whenever they have the same number of members. More precisely, sets are equipollent whenever there is a bijection between them. Equipollence is a foundational notion for Cantor's treatment of transfinite cardinal numbers.

*See* Cardinality.

**Equivalence class** A term of mathematics. Given an equivalence relation on a set, the subset of all those members which are related to a particular member $x$ is called the equivalence class of $x$. It is not hard to see that every equivalence relation on a set partitions that set into a collection of equivalence classes which, in turn, determine the equivalence relation. Example: in the Euclidean plane, the set of all lines parallel to a fixed line is the equivalence class of that line under the relation of parallelism.

**Equivalence relation** Term of mathematics. A binary relation is an equivalence relation if it is reflexive, symmetric and transitive in its field. Example: congruence is an equivalence relation on the set of Euclidean triangles.

*See* Equivalence class; Relations (properties of).

**Essentialism** The view that some properties are necessary properties of the object to which they belong. This has the consequence that some singular propositions (for example, 'Aristotle was a human being') are necessary and not just contingent truths.

**Eubulides' paradox** *See* Paradox, liar.

***Ex falso quodlibet*** Term of traditional logic, which literally means 'from the false comes anything'. Signifies that classically valid form of inference which allows one validly to conclude any proposition whatsoever from a contradiction. Forsworn by the advocates of relevance logic.

**Excluded middle** *See* Law of (the) excluded middle.

**Exclusive disjunction** *See* Disjunction.

**Existential generalization** Rule governing the logic of the existential quantifier. It permits one to conclude that there is something that has the property *P* from a premise which asserts of some particular thing that it has the property *P*.

**Existential import** The assumption made by Aristotle that every syllogistic term applies to something. Evidently Aristotle did not think that science could usefully say 'All centaurs are quadrupeds' or 'There are no Hyperboreans'. His logic thus does not admit 'empty' terms. Existential import is closely related to modern observations that in uttering 'All *S* are *P*', we ordinarily presuppose that there are *S*s. This assumption is stronger than the familiar modern one that bans empty names. For syllogistic terms are like modern predicates. It is not difficult to modify syllogistic to admit empty terms, as was first done by Schröder in 1891. (Actually, it had already been done by Leibniz, who apparently thought he must have made a mistake.) In the resulting system, the immediate inferences of subalternation and conversion *per accidens*, as well as the subaltern syllogisms and those moods which involve conversion *per accidens* (represented by mnemonics including the letter 'p'), are invalid.

**Existential instantiation** Rule governing the logic of the existential quantifier. It permits one to conclude a proposition of the form '*o* has *P*', where '*o*' is the name of an object, from the premise that 'There is at least one thing that has *P*'. In using this inference in a proof, however, one cannot choose '*o*' to be the name of any object about which one has additional information. Hence, the inference is tantamount to giving a mere name (that is, a tag which carries no descriptive information with it) to that which is said to exist.

**Existential quantifier** *See* Quantifier.

**Extension** Term of logic and linguistics. Traditionally, as applied to general terms, it signifies the set of things to which the term applies. The extension of a property $P$ is the aggregate of all items having $P$. More recently, it has come to stand for whatever thing (for example, individual, class of individuals) it is that is the semantic value of an expression under an interpretation of the language to which it belongs.

*See* Abstraction; Class; Denotation; Intension.

**Extension (of a theory)** Notion of metalogic. Let $T$ be a theory in the language $L$, $T'$ a theory in the language $L'$ and let the set of sentences of $L$ be a subset of the set of sentences of $L'$. We say that $T'$ is an extension of $T$ (or that $T$ is a subtheory of $T'$) iff $T$ is a subset of $T'$. $T'$ is then said to be a *conservative* extension of $T$ iff every sentence of $L$ that is a theorem of $T'$ is also a theorem of $T$. More generally, if we let $A$ be any set of sentences of $L$, we say that $T'$ is a conservative extension of $T$ with respect to $A$ just in case $T'$ is a subtheory of $T$ with respect to $A$. Example: first-order arithmetic with addition and multiplication is a conservative extension of first-order arithmetic with addition only.

*See* Theory.

**Extensionality, axiom of** *See* Axiom of extensionality.

# F

**Fallacy** Term of logic. A fallacy is an (often unnoticed) error or flaw in an argument which prevents it from fulfilling its persuasive task; also an argument featuring such an error. Logicians since Aristotle have constructed lists and classifications of fallacies thought to be common and especially deceptive. A fallacy is *formal* when its invalidity is discernible from the argument's structure alone. Otherwise, the fallacy counts as *informal*.

*See* Affirming the consequent, fallacy of; Ambiguity, fallacy of; Argument *ad hominem*; Argument *ad ignorantiam*; Circular reasoning, fallacy of; Composition, fallacy of; Denying the antecedent, fallacy of; Division, fallacy of; *Ignoratio elenchi*; Illicit process, fallacy of; *Non sequitur*; Paralogism.

**Fapesmo** *See* Mood (of a categorical syllogism).

**Felapto** *See* Mood (of a categorical syllogism).

**Felapton** *See* Mood (of a categorical syllogism).

**Ferio** *See* Mood (of a categorical syllogism).

**Ferison** *See* Mood (of a categorical syllogism).

**Fesapo** *See* Mood (of a categorical syllogism).

**Festino** *See* Mood (of a categorical syllogism).

**Field (of a relation/function)** Term of set theory and mathematics generally. It signifies the union of the domain and range of a relation or function.

**Figure (of a categorical syllogism)** Term of traditional logic. Signifies the relationship in which the *middle term* of a syllogism stands to its *major* and *minor terms.* Aristotle gave three figures (also called schemata). In the first, the middle term is the predicate of one of the premises and the subject of the other (that is, *S* is *M*; *M* is *P*; therefore, *S* is *P*). In the second it is the predicate of both premises (that is, *S* is *M*; *P* is *M*; therefore, *S* is *P*). In the third it is the subject of both (that is, *M* is *P*; *M* is *S*; therefore *S* is *P*). Some medievals and most moderns divided the first figure into two to get four rather than three figures. The first of these is the one given above in which the middle term is the predicate of the minor term in one of the premises and the subject of the major term in the other. In the other, the middle term is the subject of the minor term in one of the premises and the predicate of the major term in the other (that is, *P* is *M*; *M* is *S*; therefore, *S* is *P*).

*See* Perfect syllogism.

**Fimeno** *See* Mood (of a categorical syllogism).

**Finite** A term of mathematics. Standardly, a set is finite if it has *n* members for some natural number *n*.

*See* Infinite.

**Finite character** A notion of set theory and model theory, especially in application to algebra. A property *P* of sets is said to be of finite character just in case, for any set *A*, *A* has *P* if and only if every finite subset of *A* has *P*. In model theory a class of structures has finite character whenever every finitely generated substructure of any structure in the class also belongs to the class.

*See* Compactness; Structure.

**First-order/higher-order** Notions of metalogic. A first-order variable ranges over individuals (that is, the elements of the domain of an interpreting structure). A second-order variable ranges over sets of (or properties of or relations between) individuals, and a third-order variable ranges over sets of sets of (or properties of properties of, . . . ) individuals, and so on. Logic of order *n* is the logic of systems whose variables are of order at most *n*.

*See* Variable.

**Fixed point (Gödelian)** *See* Gödel sentence.

**Forcing** Semantic method for extending models of set theory. Forcing was first introduced in 1963 by Paul Cohen in his celebrated proofs of the independence from Zermelo–Fraenkel set theory of the axiom of choice and Cantor's continuum hypothesis. Since Cohen's initial results, elaborations and simplifications of forcing have been applied to obtain consistency and independence results in many branches of higher mathematics, including topology and algebra.

**Formal language** Basic notion of metalogic. A formal language is constituted by a finite vocabulary of symbols, together with formation rules for determining which strings of symbols are grammatically well formed (in particular, which are sentences). The crucial requirement is that it be effectively decidable whether a string of symbols is a well-formed expression or not.

**Formal proof** *See* Formal system.

**Formal system** Basic notion of metalogic. Also known as a logistic system or calculus, a formal system is a vehicle for carrying out absolutely rigorous proofs. This is achieved by making the concept of proof or derivation in the system a decidable one, that is, supplying a purely mechanical procedure for checking whether a putative proof is acceptable. This is done by working within a formal language and by requiring that each step in a proof should conform to a list of precisely specified rules of inference whose application is decidable. Since Frege's invention of the formal system in 1879, the idea has been extended in an obvious way to cover deductions or derivations from premises as well as proofs of theorems.

*See* Formal language.

**Foundation, axiom of** *See* Axiom of foundation.

**Fraenkel set theory** *See* Zermelo–Fraenkel set theory.

**Free (occurrence of a) variable** *See* Variable.

**Fresison** *See* Mood (of a categorical syllogism).

**Frisesomorum** *See* Mood (of a categorical syllogism).

**Function** Term of set theory and mathematics generally. Also called a mapping. A function is an operation which takes elements from one set and produces elements of another (or the same) set. If $f$ is defined on the set $A$ and produces outputs in the set $B$ then $f$ is said to be a function from $A$ to $B$ or from $A$ *into* $B$ (in symbols, $f : A \rightarrow B$); $A$ is called the *domain* of $f$ and $B$ the *range*. The elements $a$ of $A$ are called the *arguments* or *inputs* of $f$, and the element $f(a)$ of $B$ produced by applying $f$ to $a$ is called the *value* or *output* or *image* of $f$ at $a$. A *total* function from $A$ to $B$ is a function which is defined for every element of $A$. Otherwise it is a *partial* function. In set-theoretic terms, a function signifies a many-one *relation* (that is, a relation that associates with each appropriate sequence of elements of its field a unique single element of its field). An $n$-ary function $f$ is an $n+1$-ary relation $R_f$ such that for all $a_1, \ldots, a_n, c, d$ in the field of $R_f$, if $R_f(a_1, \ldots, a_n, c)$ (that is, $f(a_1, \ldots, a_n) = c$) and $R_f(a_1, \ldots, a_n, d)$, then $c = d$.

*See* Arity; Automorphism; Bijection; Choice set/function; Computable function; Constant function; Domain (of a relation/function); Endomorphism; Field (of a relation/function); Homomorphism; Identity function; Interpretation; Inverse (of a function); Isomorphism; One-one correspondence; Onto function; Projection function; Propositional function; Range (of a relation/function); Recursive function; Relation; Successor function; Truth-function; Turing computable function; Valuation.

# G

**Generalized continuum hypothesis** *See* Continuum hypothesis.

**Gödel sentence** A kind of formal sentence constructed and proved to be independent of particular theories by techniques due to Gödel. Given a formal theory $T$ that is sufficient for arithmetic, a Gödel sentence for $T$ is a sentence in the language of $T$ that 'says' it is unprovable in $T$. More precisely, a sentence $G$ is a Gödel sentence for a theory $T$ just in case the following equivalence is provable in $T$: $G \leftrightarrow \neg \mathrm{Prov}_T(\ulcorner G \urcorner)$. Such a sentence $G$ is also called a '(Gödelian) fixed point' in $T$ of the formula $\mathrm{Prov}_T(x)$. Normally, neither a Gödel sentence for $T$ nor its negation is provable in $T$.

*See* Derivability conditions.

**Gödel's theorems** *See* Completeness theorem; Incompleteness theorems.

**Greatest lower bound** *See* Bound (of a set).

**Greatest ordinal, paradox of the** *See* Paradox, Burali-Forti's.

**Grelling–Nelson paradox** *See* Paradox, Grelling's.

**Grelling's paradox** *See* Paradox, Grelling's.

# H

**Halting problem** Basic undecidability result in computability theory. It is provable that the halting problem does not admit of general solution. To solve the halting problem would be to construct a general computer program (more precisely, a Turing machine or register machine) which will correctly determine, of an arbitrary program or machine $P$ in the same language and an arbitrary potential input $n$, whether $P$'s computation will ever halt once $n$ is actually input to $P$. Part of the import of the halting problem lies in the fact that there are many natural, mathematical problems which can be shown unsolvable by comparison with it.

*See* Solvable problem.

**Hauptsatz** *See* Cut-elimination theorems.

**Heap, paradox of the** *See* Paradox, *sorites.*

**Henkin sentence** A sentence $H$ of the language of a formal theory $T$ is said to be a Henkin sentence for $T$ just in case the following is provable in $T$ (where $\mathrm{Prov}_T(x)$ satisfies the derivability conditions): $H \leftrightarrow \mathrm{Prov}_T(\ulcorner H \urcorner)$.

*See* Derivability conditions.

**Henkin's problem** A problem posed in 1952 by Leon Henkin. It can be stated as follows. Let $T$ be a standard first-order formal system of arithmetic adequate for the representation of all recursive relations of natural numbers, and let $H$ be a formula of the language of $T$, which expresses in $T$ the idea that $H$ itself is provable in $T$. Is $H$ provable in $T$ or independent of $T$? Henkin's problem was solved by Löb in 1955. He showed that any such $H$ is provable in $T$.

*See* Henkin sentence; Löb's theorem.

**Herbrand's theorem** Fundamental normal form result of proof theory, first stated by Herbrand in his 1929 thesis. One may conceive of the theorem as a constructive version of the Löwenheim–Skolem theorem. In a special case, Herbrand's theorem asserts that an existential sentence is a theorem of classical predicate logic if and only if there is a quasi-tautology composed solely of instances of the quantifier-free matrix of the sentence. Here, a quasi-tautology is a tautological consequence of the axioms of identity.

**Heterologicality, paradox of** *See* Paradox, Grelling's.

**Higher-order** *See* First-order/higher-order.

**Homomorphism** Term of algebra and model theory. In mathematics generally, a homomorphism is (1) a function from the domain or universe of a structure *A* into the domain of a structure *B* of the same type or signature which (2) preserves structural features relevant to the signature. More specifically, a homomorphism maps the distinguished elements, relations and operations of *A* into corresponding elements, relations and operations of *B*. In formal logic, a homomorphism is a structure-preserving function between similar models.

*See* Endomorphism; Isomorphism.

**Horned syllogism** *See* Dilemma.

**Hypothetical syllogism** *See* Syllogism, hypothetical.

# I

**Identity function** The identity function maps every element to itself: for all $x$, $I(x) = x$.

*See* Recursive function.

**Identity, law of** *See* Law of identity.

**Identity of indiscernibles** Principle enunciated by Leibniz (*Discourse on Metaphysics*, §9). It states that two substances may not be exactly alike in all qualitative respects and differ only numerically. Stated contrapositively and in more modern terms, it says that for every property $P$ and all individuals $x$ and $y$, if $x$ has $P$ if and only if $y$ has $P$, then $x$ is identical to $y$.

*See* Indiscernibility of identicals.

***Ignoratio elenchi*** Term of traditional logic. Signifies a type of fallacy in which an arguer claims to have proved something but has at best proved something else.

**Illicit process, fallacy of** A fallacious type of syllogistic reasoning in which a term is distributed in the conclusion but not in the premises. If the major term is undistributed, it is called a fallacy of illicit major term (for example, 'All men are mortal, no women are men; therefore, no women are mortal'). If the minor term is undistributed, it is called a fallacy of illicit minor term (for example, 'All men are mortal, no women are men; therefore, no mortals are women').

*See* Distributed term (of a syllogism).

**Image (of a function)** *See* Function.

**Immediate inference** A valid one-premise argument, particularly in Aristotelian logic. Aristotle focuses on syllogisms, that is, two-premise arguments from categorical propositions. But in reducing imperfect syllogisms to the (perfect) first figure, he also employs some modes of immediate inference: conversion (simple), conversion *per accidens* and *reductio ad absurdum*. Elsewhere he also recognizes obversion, contraposition and subalternation.

**Implication, logical** Basic term of logic. A set of propositions $A$ is said to logically imply a proposition $p$ just in case it is impossible that all the elements of $A$ be true and $p$ false.

**Implication, material** *See* Paradoxes of material and strict implication.

**Implication, strict** *See* Paradoxes of material and strict implication.

**Impredicative definition** Term of metalogic. An impredicative definition of an object or class is any definition that refers to a collection of which that object or class is an element. The use of impredicative definitions in mathematics was forsworn by Russell in his vicious-circle principle. The enforcement of this principle was the primary motive of his theory of types.

**Inaccessible cardinal** *See* Large cardinal.

**Inclusive disjunction** *See* Disjunction.

**Incompleteness theorems** Common name for two theorems first published by Gödel in 1931. The first of these says (roughly) that, if $T$ is a consistent, recursively axiomatizable theory that includes an elementary fragment of arithmetic, then there is a sentence $G$ of the language of $T$ such that neither $G$ nor $\neg G$ is provable in $T$. The second says (roughly) that, if $T$ is a consistent, recursively axiomatizable theory that includes an elementary fragment of arithmetic, then there is a formula $\mathrm{Con}_T$ of the language of $T$ which expresses the idea that $T$ is consistent and which is not provable in $T$.

*See* Gödel sentence.

**Inconsistent triad** *See* Antilogism.

**Indefinite categorical proposition** *See* Categorical proposition.

**Indemonstrables** The five basic rules of Stoic propositional logic, called 'indemonstrable' (literally, 'undemonstrated') because they were not in need of proof.

**Independence** Basic notion of logic and axiomatics. Typically, a proposition $p$ is said to be independent of a set of propositions $A$ just in case $p$ is not logically implied by $A$. A set of sentences may then be said to be independent (or its elements mutually independent) if none of its elements is logically implied by the remaining elements. Independence in this sense has commonly been identified as a virtue of an axiomatic system by modern foundational thinkers. In another sense of independence, a proposition $p$ is said to be independent of a set of propositions $A$ just in case neither $p$ nor $\neg p$ is logically implied by $A$.

**Indirect proof** *See Reductio ad absurdum.*

**Indiscernibility of identicals** Converse of Leibniz's principle of the identity of indiscernibles formulated in such famous texts of modern logic as Frege's *Begriffsschrift* (1879). It states that for all individuals $x$ and $y$ and all properties $P$, if $x$ and $y$ are identical, then $x$ has $P$ if and only if $y$ has $P$. A first-order version not quantifying over properties can be written in symbolic notation as

$$\forall x \forall y (x = y \rightarrow (Px \leftrightarrow Py)).$$

**Induction, mathematical** Fundamental principle or form of mathematical reasoning for the natural numbers, variants of which apply to other well-ordered or recursively defined collections. For the natural numbers, induction allows one to conclude that every number has a property $P$ from the premises that 0 has $P$ and that, whenever a number has $P$, so does its successor. A variant, known as 'complete induction' or 'course-of-values', or *strong* induction, allows one to conclude that every number has a property $P$ from the premise that any number is such that it has $P$ whenever all its predecessors do.

*See* Axiom schema; Peano postulates; Transfinite induction.

**Inference** Basic term of logic. Used to signify either an argument, an individual step in an argument or the process of passing from belief in or assertion of the premises of an argument to belief in or assertion of its conclusion. In this latter sense, an inference requires both belief in the premises and belief that the premises support the conclusion.

*See* Adjunction; Ampliation; Contraction; Contraposition; Conversion *per accidens*; Conversion, simple; Derivation; Dilution; *Ex falso quodlibet*; Existential generalization; Existential instantiation; Immediate inference; Laws of thought; *Modus ponens*; *Modus tollens*; Obversion; *Reductio ad absurdum*; Subalternation; Universal generalization; Universal instantiation; Validity.

***Infimum*** *See* Bound (of a set).

**Infinite** A term of mathematics. Standardly, a set is infinite when it is not finite, that is, when it stands in one-one correspondence with no bounded set of natural numbers. In a set theory which includes an axiom of choice, this is tantamount to taking a set to be infinite whenever it has a subset in one-one correspondence with the entire collection of natural numbers. Dedekind defined a set to be infinite when it could be put into one-one correspondence with a proper subset of itself.

*See* Finite.

**Infinity, axiom of** *See* Axiom of infinity.

**Injection** *See* One-one correspondence.

**Input (of a function)** *See* Function.

**Intension** Term of logic and linguistics. The contemporary term 'intension' derives from the traditional logical term 'comprehension'. According to Arnauld and Nicole in their *Port-Royal Logic* (1662), the *comprehension* of a general idea or term is the set of all attributes or properties it entails. Comprehension in the semantic sense has proved perennially useful, for example, in Kant's definition of analyticity and in

Montague's treatment of universal noun phrases ('all men'). During the nineteenth century, 'intension' supplanted 'comprehension' for the non-extensional counterpart of 'extension'.

*See* Connotation; Extension; Lekton.

**Interpretation** Term of mathematical logic and linguistics. Logicians use the term 'interpretation' for a variety of distinct conceptions. First, in semantics, an interpretation of a formal language is a function (or other mathematical setting) sufficient to determine meanings or denotations for all grammatically correct expressions of the language. For formal propositional logic, a semantic interpretation is an assignment of truth-values to atomic formulas extendible recursively to all formulas in accordance with the truth tables for the connectives. In quantifier logics, interpretations in this sense are functions assigning denotations to each of the nonlogical symbols of the language. Alternatively, 'interpretation' sometimes refers to assignments of truth-conditions to all formulas of a quantifier language. It is also sometimes used in a syntactic sense to describe mappings of one formal language (or of one formal theory) into another that preserve certain of their important characteristics.

*See* Satisfaction; Valuation.

**Intersection (of sets)** Operation of set or class theory. Given sets $A$ and $B$, their intersection $A \cap B$ is the set containing just those members common to both $A$ and $B$.

**Into function** *See* Function.

**Inverse (of a function)** Term of set theory and mathematics generally. The inverse of a one-one function $f : A \rightarrow B$ is the function $f^{-1} : B \rightarrow A$ that is obtained by 'reversing' $f$. Thus for each $a$ in $A$ and each $b$ in $B$, if $f(a) = b$, then $f^{-1}(b) = a$. The domain of $f^{-1}$ is thus the range of $f$ and its range is that class of elements of the domain of $f$ for which $f$ has a value. (If a function is not one-one then its inverse cannot be defined.)

**Inverse (of a relation)** *See* Converse (of a relation).

**Irreflexive relation/order** *See* Relations (properties of).

**Isomorphism** Term of set theory, model theory and mathematics generally. An isomorphism between two structures $A$ and $B$ of the same type or signature is a bijection $f : A \rightarrow B$ from the domain (or universe) of $A$ to the domain of $B$ which preserves structure. If $R_A xy$ for elements $x, y$ of $A$, then $R_B f(x) f(y)$, where $R_B$ is the relation in $B$ which corresponds to the relation $R_A$ in $A$. And if $g_A : A \rightarrow A$ and $g_B : B \rightarrow B$ are corresponding functions defined on $A$ and $B$, respectively, then $f(g_A(a)) = g_B(f(a))$ for all $a$ in $A$. In formal logic, an isomorphism is such a correspondence between similar models. Example: the function 'multiplication by 2' is an isomorphism between the structure of the natural numbers $\{0, 1, 2, \ldots\}$ together with the operation of addition, and the set $\{0, 2, 4, \ldots\}$ with the same operation. This function is *one-one* because every number in the set $\{0, 2, 4, \ldots\}$ corresponds to a unique natural number (found by dividing by 2). It is *onto* because every number in the set $\{0, 2, 4, \ldots\}$ is the image of some natural number. And it is structure-preserving because it maps the zero element of the natural numbers to the zero element of the set $\{0, 2, 4, \ldots\}$ and for all natural numbers $n, m$, $2(n + m) = 2n + 2m$.

*See* Automorphism; Homomorphism.

# J

**Join** Term of set theory and mathematics generally. The join of a family of sets is their union. In geometry, the join of two points is a line.

*See* Union (of sets).

**Joint denial** Term of logic. Refers to a logical operation on propositions that is of the type of the English operator 'It is neither the case that... nor the case that ___'. In symbolic systems it is commonly represented by '∅'. Compounds formed from such an operator are true just in case both of their component sentences are false. Joint denial is one of two single propositional operators that is, by itself, a complete set of connectives.

*See* Complete set of connectives.

# K

**Kleene's second recursion theorem** *See* Recursion theorem.

**König's lemma** A title shared by two distinct, fundamental results in set theory proved by two different mathematicians. The earlier 'König's lemma' was propounded for powers of cardinal numbers by Julius König in 1905 and, in its contemporary formulation, implies that the cardinality of the set of real numbers cannot be the first limit aleph. The second, also known as 'König's infinity lemma', was proved by Denes König in 1927 and is commonly stated as a principle for treelike orderings: a finitely branching tree with infinitely many nodes must contain at least one branch of infinite length. Gödel employed this latter lemma in his proof of the completeness of first-order logic. In classical set theory, the infinity lemma entails the topological compactness of Cantor space and the compactness property of classical propositional logic.

*See* Alephs; Continuum hypothesis.

# L

**Large cardinal** Concept of abstract set theory. As hypothesized by set theorists, the various families of large cardinals include compact cardinals, inaccessible cardinals, Mahlo cardinals and measurable cardinals. For example, an *inaccessible* cardinal (or *strongly inaccessible* cardinal) is a cardinal closed under the operation of taking power sets in the sense that, if $A$ is inaccessible and $B$ is of lesser cardinality than $A$, then the power set of $B$ is also of lesser cardinality than $A$. Since the existence of inaccessible cardinals would imply that Zermelo–Fraenkel set theory is consistent, that theory is, by Gödel's second incompleteness theorem, insufficient to prove their existence. Large cardinals are studied (following a suggestion of Gödel) as potential avenues to the discovery of new axioms for set theory sufficient to settle outstanding questions such as the continuum problem.

*See* Continuum hypothesis.

**Law of comparability** *See* Law of trichotomy.

**Law of contradiction** Also known as the law of noncontradiction. The title refers to a variety of logical, semantic and metaphysical principles, salient among them (1) a principle of propositional semantics and (2) a traditional 'law of thought' propounded by Plato in his *Republic* and accepted by Aristotle. In case (1) the law of contradiction affirms that no single statement can be both true and false at the same time. In Plato's formulation (2), it asserts that a single thing cannot have contrary properties in the same part of itself, at the same time and in the same respect.

*See* Laws of thought.

**Law of (the) excluded middle** Also known as the '*tertium non datur*', the title refers to a variety of logical, semantic and metaphysical principles, among them (1) a well-known law of propositional reasoning and (2) a traditional 'law of thought,' set out by Aristotle in his *Metaphysics*. In case (1), the law of excluded middle affirms that, for any statement *S*, the claim '*S* or not *S*' is logically true. (The law of excluded middle, so understood, should be distinguished from the semantic principle of bivalence.) One version of the law of excluded middle in Aristotle denies that there is anything intermediate between the two halves of a contradiction.

*See* Bivalence; Laws of thought.

**Law of identity** A title applied to a variety of logical, semantic and metaphysical claims, prominent among them (1) a law of propositional logic, (2) a basic principle in the logic of identity and (3) a traditional 'law of thought'. The principle of propositional logic known as the law of identity asserts that 'If *p* then *p*' is logically true. In the theory of identity, the claims that '*a* equals *a*' is always true and that every thing is self-identical are treated as laws of identity. Among so-called laws of thought, the 'law of identity' refers, in addition, to the metaphysical principle that everything is what it is and not something else.

*See* Laws of thought.

**Law of trichotomy** Also called the law of comparability. In general, a division of entities into three sets that are pairwise disjoint (that is, non-overlapping) and exhaustive. In the theory of real numbers, for example, the law of trichotomy is the statement that, for any numbers *r* and *s*, either *r* is less than *s* or *s* is less than *r* or *r* equals *s*. Although counted a fundamental property of the real numbers in classical mathematics, constructivists and Brouwerian intuitionists reject this principle of trichotomy. In set theory, the law of trichotomy asserts a similar comparability property for sets with respect to cardinality: for any sets *A* and *B*, either *A* has cardinality less than *B*, or *B* less than *A*, or *A* and *B* have the same cardinality.

**Laws of thought** Term of traditional logic used to refer to a family of principles that were taken to be laws according to which valid inference proceeds regardless of the subject matter involved. The three principles most commonly identified as belonging to this family are: *the law of identity* (taken as stating (1) that every thing is identical to itself or (2) that every proposition implies itself), *the law of contradiction* (taken as stating (1) that nothing both has and lacks a given attribute or (2) that no proposition is both true and false), and *the law of the excluded middle* (taken as stating (1) that every thing either has or lacks a given property or (2) that every proposition is either true or false).

*See* Law of contradiction; Law of (the) excluded middle; Law of identity.

**Least upper bound** *See* Bound (of a set).

**Left field (of a relation)** *See* Domain (of a relation/function).

**Lekton** The Stoic term for what is meant or signified by a sign, as opposed to the physical object it is about; in modern parlance (roughly), the sense or *intension* of the sign. *Lekta* may be *complete* (propositions) or *deficient* (qualities signified by subject and predicate). Complete *lekta* are the bearers of truth and falsity. *Lekta* were taken to be not bodies but real non-physical things expressed by a sign and apprehended by us when we think.

*See* Intension.

**Lemma, König's** *See* König's lemma.

**Lemma, Zorn's** *See* Zorn's lemma.

**Liar paradox** *See* Paradox, liar.

**Limit ordinal** Term of set theory and mathematics generally. It signifies any non-zero ordinal that has no immediate predecessor. (An ordinal that has an immediate predecessor is often referred to as a 'successor ordinal'.)

*See* Predecessor; Successor.

**Limitation of size** *See* Von Neumann–Bernays–Gödel set theory.

**Linear relation/order** *See* Ordering; Relations (properties of).

**Löb's theorem** Important result in the metamathematics of formal theories, especially, of arithmetic. Proved in 1955 by M.H. Löb as a solution to Henkin's problem. The theorem showed that for any theory *T*, any formula $\mathrm{Prov}_T(x)$ of the language of *T* that satisfies the derivability conditions, and any formula *A* of the language of *T*, if '$\mathrm{Prov}_T(\ulcorner A \urcorner) \rightarrow A$' is a theorem of *T*, then so is *A*. (Less formally: if *T* proves that *A* is implied by a formula expressing its provability-in-*T*, then *T* proves *A*.) If one accepts the derivability conditions as conditions that must be satisfied by any formula $\mathrm{Prov}_T(x)$ of the language of *T* that is capable of expressing the notion of provability-in-*T*, then Löb's theorem answers Henkin's problem in the affirmative. Any sentence that asserts its own provability-in-*T* is provable in *T*.

*See* Derivability conditions; Henkin's problem.

**Logical constant** *See* Constant.

**Logical implication** *See* Implication, logical.

**Logistic system** *See* Formal system.

**Löwenheim–Skolem theorem(s)** Basic theorem proved by Löwenheim in 1915 and Skolem in 1919, showing that any theory in first-order logic (with identity) that has a model has a countable model. Tarski (1928) later showed that every such theory that has an infinite model has a model of every infinite cardinality. The original theorem shows that some theories (for example, set theory and the theory of real numbers) have unexpectedly small models and is therefore sometimes referred to as the *downward* Löwenheim–Skolem theorem.

The theorem proved by Tarski indicates that theories with infinite models have unexpectedly large models and is sometimes called the *upward* Löwenheim–Skolem theorem.

*See* Herbrand's theorem.

**Lower bound** *See* Bound (of a set).

# M

**Mahlo cardinal** *See* Large cardinal.

**Major premise (of a syllogism)** Term of traditional logic designating the premise, in a categorical syllogism, containing the major term (that is, the term that is the predicate of the conclusion). For example, in the Barbara syllogism 'All mammals are vertebrates; all whales are mammals; therefore, all whales are vertebrates,' 'vertebrate' is the major term and 'All mammals are vertebrates' the major premise.

*See* Major term (of a syllogism); Syllogism, categorical.

**Major term (of a syllogism)** Term of traditional logic. The predicate term of the conclusion of a categorical syllogism. In general, the predicate term of any categorical proposition is called the major term.

*See* Categorical proposition; Syllogism, categorical.

**Many-valued logics** Propositional logics which study the logic of truth-functional propositional operators admitting more than the two classical truth-values 'true' and 'false'.

**Mapping (map)** *See* Function.

**Markov's principle** Named for Russian mathematician A.A. Markov. It is a law governing sets or predicates of numbers in various forms of constructive mathematics. Markov first proposed it in 1952 or 1953 under the title 'principle of constructive choices'; it remains characteristic of mathematical constructivism in the Russian or Markovian school of logicians. Generously formulated, Markov's principle states that, whenever a set of natural numbers is decidable and it is false that all numbers belong to it, then some number fails to be its member. Although a theorem of classical logic, it is underivable in many formalisms for constructive mathematics and is rejected by intuitionists who follow Brouwer.

**Material implication** *See* Paradoxes of material and strict implication.

**Maximal consistent set** Notion of metalogic. If $A$ is a set of sentences of a language $L$, $A$ is said to be maximal consistent just in case (1) $A$ is consistent, and (2) no further sentence of $L$ can be added to $A$ to form a consistent set.

**Measurable cardinal** *See* Large cardinal.

**Meet** Term of set theory and mathematics generally. The meet of a family of sets is their intersection. In geometry, the point of intersection of two lines is often referred to as their meet.

*See* Intersection (of sets).

**Middle term (of a syllogism)** Term of traditional logic. The term that appears in each of the premises but not in the conclusion of a categorical syllogism.

*See* Syllogism, categorical.

**Minor premise (of a syllogism)** Term of traditional logic designating the premise, in a categorical syllogism, containing the minor term, that is, the term which is the subject of the conclusion. For example, in the Barbara syllogism 'All mammals are vertebrates; all whales are mammals; therefore, all whales are vertebrates', 'whale' is the minor term and 'All whales are mammals' the minor premise.

*See* Minor term (of a syllogism); Syllogism, categorical.

**Minor term (of a syllogism)** Term of traditional logic. The subject term of the conclusion of a categorical syllogism. In general, the subject term of any categorical proposition is called the minor term.

*See* Categorical proposition; Syllogism, categorical.

**Mnemonics, syllogistic** The mnemonic names for the syllogistic moods (valid forms of syllogism) were established by the early thirteenth century. An early fairly complete list is given by Peter of Spain (*Summulae logicales* 4.17). The names encode the way to reduce the syllogisms to the first figure, following Aristotle. The significant letters in the mnemonics are the initial consonant, the first three vowels and 's', 'p', 'm' and 'c'. Syllogisms whose names begin with 'B' reduce to Barbara; with 'C' to Celarent; with 'D' to Darii; and with 'F' to Ferio. The vowels 'a', 'e', 'i' and 'o' denote the four forms of categorical proposition. The consonant 's' after a vowel indicates a *simple* conversion of the corresponding first-figure proposition; 'p' indicates conversion *per accidens*, which presupposes existential import; 'm' indicates *mutatio praemissarum*, that is, interchange of the premises; and 'c' indicates indirect proof, *per contradictionem*. (Subalternation, a mode of immediate inference recognized by Aristotle that also presupposes existential import, is not indicated, for the so-called subaltern moods were codified only later.) Example: to reduce a second-figure syllogism in the mood Camestrop to the first-figure mood Celarent, we interchange the premises (m), convert the *E*-premise simply (s), and convert the *E*-conclusion *per accidens* (p) to the desired *O*-conclusion.

*See* Categorical proposition; Conversion *per accidens*; Conversion, simple; Existential import; Figure (of a categorical syllogism); Mood (of a categorical syllogism).

**Modal syllogism** *See* Syllogism, modal.

**Model** *See* Structure.

***Modus ponendo tollens*** Term of traditional logic. Signifies that basic mood or form of the disjunctive syllogism in which one premise is an exclusive disjunction, the other one of its disjuncts and the conclusion the denial of the remaining disjunct. Hence, it is either of the form '*P* (excl.) or *Q*. *P*. Therefore not *Q*' or of the form '*P* (excl.) or *Q*. *Q*. Therefore not *P*'.

***Modus ponens*** Term of traditional logic and modern logic (in full, *modus ponendo ponens*). Traditionally, *modus ponens* is one of the basic forms or moods of the mixed hypothetical syllogism; namely, that in which the minor premise is the antecedent of the major premise and the conclusion its consequent. In other words, it is the following argument form: 'If *p* then *q*. *p* ∴ *q*'. It is also used as the name for the rule of inference which allows one to infer '*q*' from the two propositions 'If *p* then *q*' and '*p*'.

***Modus tollendo ponens*** Term of traditional logic. Signifies the basic form or mood of the disjunctive syllogism in which one premise is an exclusive disjunction, the other the denial of one of its disjuncts and the conclusion the remaining disjunct. Hence, it is either of the form '*P* (excl.) or *Q*. Not *P*. Therefore *Q*' or '*P* (excl.) or *Q*. Not *Q*. Therefore *P*'.

***Modus tollens*** Term of traditional logic (in full, *modus tollendo tollens*). *Modus tollens* signifies the basic form or mood of the mixed hypothetical syllogism in which the minor premise is the denial of the consequent of the major premise and whose conclusion is the denial of its antecedent. In other words, it is the following argument form: 'If *p* then *q*. Not *q* ∴ not *p*'. It is also used as the name for the rule of inference which allows one to infer 'Not *p*' from the two propositions 'If *p* then *q*' and 'Not *q*'.

**Mood (of a categorical syllogism)** Term of traditional logic. The moods are the different valid syllogistic forms that are available within a given figure through variation of the quantities (universal or particular) and qualities (affirmative or negative) of the premises and conclusion. As an example, consider the figure '*A* is *B*, *C* is *A* ∴ *C* is *B*' (where *B* is the major, *C* the minor and *A* the middle term). It has the following moods:

(1) 'Every *A* is *B*, every *C* is *A* ∴ every *C* is *B*',

(2) 'No *A* is *B*, every *C* is *A* ∴ no *C* is *B*',

(3) 'Every *A* is *B*, some *C* is *A* ∴ some *C* is *B*' and

(4) 'No *A* is *B*, some *C* is *A* ∴ some *C* is not *B*'.

In the first figure, then, (1) is in the mood *AAA* (Barbara), (2) in the mood *EAE* (Celarent), (3) in the mood *AII* (Darii) and (4) in the mood *EIO* (Ferio). The moods listed below have been recognized under the mnemonic name given. (Roman numerals indicate figures; the letters '*a*', '*e*', '*i*' and '*o*' stand for the quantified copulas of the four categorical forms of proposition. The major premise is given first.)

Bamana IV. $SaM, MaP \therefore SaP$ (Barbara with interchanged premises, recognized as a separate mood by Peter of Mantua (1483) and Peter Tartaret (1503).)

Baralipton I. $MaS, PaM \therefore SiP$ (Bramantip with interchanged premises; one of the new 'first figure' syllogisms attributed to Theophrastus.)

Barbara I. $MaP, SaM \therefore SaP$

Barbari I. $MaP, SaM \therefore SiP$ (subaltern mood)

Baroco II. $PaM, SoM \therefore SoP$

Bocardo III. $MoP, MaS \therefore SoP$

Bramantip (Bamalip) IV. $PaM, MaS \therefore SiP$

Camene IV. $SaM, MeP \therefore SeP$ (Celarent with interchanged premises, recognized as a separate mood by Peter of Mantua (1483) and Peter Tartaret (1503).)

Camenes (Calemes) IV. $PaM, MeS \therefore SeP$

Camenop (Calemop, Calemos) IV. $PaM, MeS \therefore SoP$ (A subaltern mood, although it does not require subalternation for its reduction.)

Camestres II. $PaP, SeM \therefore SeP$

Camestrop (Camestros) II. $PaM, SeM \therefore SoP$ (A subaltern mood, although it does not require subalternation for its reduction.)

Celantes I. $MeS.PaM \therefore SeP$ (Camenes with interchanged premises; one of the new 'first figure' syllogisms attributed to Theophrastus.)

Celantos (properly 'Celantop') I. $MeS, PaM \therefore SoP$ (Mnemonic name given by Peter of Mantua (1483) for the syllogistic mood Camenop with interchanged premises. It should properly be called 'Celantop'. It is the sort of new 'first figure' syllogism discovered by Theophrastus, but he seems to have missed this one, probably because it is a subaltern mood.)

Celarent I. $MeP, SaM \therefore SeP$

Celaront (Celaro) I. $MeP, SaM \therefore SoP$ (subaltern mood)

Cesare II. $PeM, SaM \therefore SeP$

Cesaro II. $PeM, SaM \therefore SoP$ (subaltern mood)

Dabitis I. $MaS, PiM \therefore SiP$ (Dimaris with interchanged premises; one of the new 'first figure' syllogisms attributed to Theophrastus.)

Darapti III. $MaP, MaS \therefore SiP$ (Darapti is of interest because it enables us to prove existential import – some *A* are *A* – for an arbitrary term *A*, from the logical truth that all *A* are *A*, which, however, is not mentioned by Aristotle.)

Daraptis $MaS, MaP \therefore SiP$ (Darapti with interchanged premises, recognized as a separate mood by Galen (*c.* AD 170). Daraptis stands to the third figure as the Theophrastian moods to the fourth figure.)

Darii I. $MaP, SiM \therefore SiP$

Datisi III. $MaP, MiS \therefore SiP$

Dimari IV. $SiM, MaP \therefore SiP$ (Darii with interchanged premises, recognized as a separate mood by Peter of Mantua (1483) and Peter Tartaret (1503).)

Dimaris (Dimatis) IV. $PiM, MaS \therefore SiP$

Disamis III. $MiP, MaS \therefore SiP$

Fapesmo I. $MaS, PeM \therefore SoP$ (Fesapo with interchanged premises; one of the new 'first figure' syllogisms attributed to Theophrastus.)

Felapton (Felapto) III. $MeP, MaS \therefore SiP$

Ferio I. $MeP, SiM \therefore SoP$

Ferison III. $MeP, MiS \therefore SiP$

Fesapo IV. $PeM, MaS \therefore SoP$

Festino II. $PeM, SiM \therefore SoP$

Fimeno IV. $SiM, MeP \therefore SoP$ (Ferio with interchanged premises, recognized as a separate mood by Peter of Mantua (1483) and Peter Tartaret (1503).)

Fresison IV. $PeM, MiS \therefore SoP$

Frisesomorum I. $MiS, PeM \therefore SoP$ (Fresison with interchanged premises; one of the new 'first figure' syllogisms attributed to Theophrastus.)

*See* Categorical proposition; Figure (of a categorical syllogism); Mnemonics, syllogistic; Perfect syllogism; Subalternation.

**Multiplicative axiom** *See* Axiom of choice.

# N

**Negation** Notion of propositional logic. Signifies either an operator that is used to negate the truth of propositions or a compound proposition formed by applying such an operator to a proposition. The negation of a sentence has the opposite truth-value of the sentence negated. In English, negation is expressed by 'It is not the case that' and cognate phrases.

**Negation-completeness** *See* Completeness (of a theory).

**Negative (proposition)** *See* Categorical proposition.

**Neumann–Bernays–Gödel set theory** *See* Von Neumann–Bernays–Gödel set theory.

***Non sequitur*** Term of logic; a fallacy or class of fallacies. Any argument or inference in which the conclusion does not follow correctly from the premises.

**Noncontradiction, law of** *See* Law of contradiction.

**Nonstandard model** Term of metalogic. A model for a theory is nonstandard if it is not isomorphic to the intended model. Examples: first-order arithmetic has nonstandard models, but second-order arithmetic does not.

**Normal form (conjunctive)** Notion of formal logic. A formula is in conjunctive normal form if it is a conjunction of disjunctions of atomic formulas and negations of atomic formulas. In classical propositional logic, every formula is logically equivalent to one in conjunctive normal form.

**Normal form (disjunctive)** Notion of formal logic. A formula is in disjunctive normal form if it is a disjunction of conjunctions of atomic formulas and negations of atomic formulas. In classical propositional logic, every formula is logically equivalent to one in disjunctive normal form.

**Normal form (prenex)** Notion of metalogic. A formula is said to be in prenex normal form if it consists of a (possibly empty) string of quantifiers (called its quantifier prefix) followed by a formula (called its matrix) that contains no quantifiers. Every formula of a first-order language is logically equivalent to a first-order formula in prenex normal form.

**Normal form (Skolem)** Notion of metalogic. A formula is said to be in Skolem normal form when it is in prenex normal form and its quantifier prefix consists of a (possibly empty) block of existential quantifiers followed by a (possibly empty) block of universal quantifiers. A formula and its Skolem normal form are either both provable or both not provable in the predicate calculus and, so, either both valid or both not valid.

**N-tuple** *See* -Tuple.

**Null set** *See* Empty set.

# O

**Obversion** Term of traditional logic. Signifies four valid modes of immediate inference recognized by Aristotle and supporting equivalences:

'All *A* are *B*; therefore no *A* are non-*B*';

'No *A* are *B*; therefore all *A* are non-*B*';

'Some *A* are *B*; therefore some *A* are not non-*B*';

'Some *A* are not *B*; therefore some *A* are non-*B*'.

*See* Immediate inference.

**Omega** Symbol from set theory. A lowercase omega ($\omega$) was used by Cantor and later set theorists to denote a least infinite ordinal number, that of the set of natural numbers under their usual ordering.

**Omega-completeness** Notion of metamathematics. A theory $T$ in an arithmetic language $L$ is said to be omega-complete (usually written '$\omega$-complete') just in case for every formula $\phi x$ of $L$, if every formula of the form $\phi n$ (where '$n$' is a numeral) is provable in $T$, then so is the formula $\forall x \phi x$.

**Omega-consistency** Notion of metamathematics. A theory $T$ in an arithmetic language $L$ is said to be omega-consistent (usually written '$\omega$-consistent') if there is no formula $\phi x$ of $L$ such that each formula of the form $\phi n$ (where '$n$' is a numeral) is provable in $T$ and $T$ also proves $\neg\forall x \phi x$. Gödel used $\omega$-consistency as a condition on the theories for which he proved his incompleteness theorems. Rosser later showed how to prove the first incompleteness theorem using just consistency (a weaker condition than omega-consistency).

*See* Consistency.

**One-one correspondence** Term of set theory and mathematics generally. Also called an injection. A one-one (or 1-1) correspondence between two sets $A$ and $B$ is a function $f : A \rightarrow B$ which maps every element of $A$ to a unique element of $B$: for all $x, y$ in $A$, if $f(x) = f(y)$, then $x = y$.

**Onto function** Term of set theory and mathematics generally. Also called a surjection. A function $f : A \rightarrow B$ is said to be *onto B* when every element of $B$ is the value of $f$ for some element of $A$: for all $b$ in $B$, $b = f(a)$ for some $a$ in $A$.

**Open term/formula** *See* Variable.

**Opposition** Term of traditional logic. Aristotle used 'opposition' as a general term for the different ways in which categorical propositions could be at odds with one another. He delineated three species of opposition: contradictories, contraries and subcontraries. Contradictories cannot both be true and cannot both be false. Contraries cannot both be true but can both be false. Subcontraries cannot both be false but can both be true. These relations were captured in the famous *square of opposition*, a post-Aristotelian device which arranged the *A, E, I* and *O* propositions as follows. The proposition-types in the top row (that is, *A* and *E*) are contraries, the proposition-types of the bottom row (that is, *I* and *O*) subcontraries, and the diagonal pairs (that is, *A* and *O*, and *E* and *I*) are contradictories.

| | |
|---|---|
| Universal affirmative (*A*)<br>All *A* are *B* | Universal negative (*E*)<br>No *A* are *B* |
| Particular affirmative (*I*)<br>Some *A* are *B* | Particular negative (*O*)<br>Some *A* are not *B* |

*See* Categorical proposition.

**Order** *See* Ordering.

**Ordering** Term of set theory and mathematics generally. An ordering (or order) is a relation defined on a set which allows at least certain elements of that set to be arranged in order. A relation $R$ defined on a set $A$ yields a *partial* ordering if it is reflexive, antisymmetric and transitive on $A$. $R$ is said to be a *total* ordering, a *linear* ordering or simply an ordering of $A$ if it is connected, irreflexive and transitive in $A$. Examples: the 'subset of' relation gives a partial order on the power set of a set. The 'less than' relation is a total order of the natural numbers.

*See* Quasi-ordering; Relations (properties of); Well-ordering.

**Order type** Term of set theory and mathematics generally. Two ordered sets are said to have the same order type just in case they are isomorphic in the following sense. If the set $A$ is ordered by a relation $R$ and the set $B$ is ordered by the relation $S$, $A$ and $B$ have the same order type if there is a bijection $f: A \rightarrow B$ such that for any $x, y$ in $A$, $Rxy$ if and only if $Sf(x)f(y)$. Two sets with the same order type are also said to be *similar*.

**Ordered n-tuple** *See* -Tuple.

**Ordered pair** An ordered pair is an ordered $n$-tuple with $n = 2$.

*See* -Tuple.

**Ordinal (number)** Term of set theory and mathematics generally. The cardinal number of a collection is concerned only with its 'size', but the ordinal is concerned also with the relationship of its elements. (Cantor pointed out that the differences between these two ways of measuring class size become significant when one is dealing with infinite or transfinite sets.) The ordinal numbers are generally defined as the order types of the well-ordered sets. So two sets have the same ordinal if there is an isomorphism between them. Intuitively, ordinals measure the size of a collection by determining how far into a given 'indexing' set one has to go in order to count its members.

*See* Cardinality; Limit ordinal; Order type.

**Output (of a function)** *See* Function.

# P

**Pairing axiom** *See* Axiom of pairing.

**Paradox, Berry's** A simplified variant of Richard's paradox first published in a paper of Russell's in 1906 and attributed to the philosopher George Berry. Consider the least natural number not definable in fewer than twelve words; this number is itself here defined in fewer than twelve words, a contradiction. (Since the number of descriptions less than twelve words long in the English language must be finite, and the set of natural numbers is infinite, there must be at least one natural number which cannot be identified with a twelve-word description of itself, so the least such natural number is well-defined.)

*See* Paradox, Richard's.

**Paradox, Burali-Forti's** Also called the paradox of the greatest ordinal. The ordinal numbers, considered in their natural order, form a well-ordered collection, which thus has an ordinal, $\Omega$. But the ordinal number of a sequence of ordinals is greater than every ordinal in the sequence. Hence, $\Omega$ is greater than every ordinal and so cannot be an ordinal.

**Paradox, Cantor's** A set-theoretic paradox first discovered by Cantor. If the collection $U$ of all sets itself constitutes a set, then, by Cantor's theorem, its power set $\wp(U)$ must be larger than it is. But, by definition, $\wp(U)$ is itself a collection of sets and, hence, must be contained in $U$, a contradiction. In contemporary set theory, this result is taken to show that the universe of all sets cannot be a set but must be considered a proper class.

**Paradox, Curry's** Paradox formulated by H.B. Curry in 1942. Consider the following sentence, $A$: 'If this sentence is true, then $B$'. If $A$ is true, then if $A$ is true then $B$. Eliminating the repetition of the antecedent, we infer that if $A$ is true then $B$, hence that $A$ is true, and finally, by *modus ponens*, we conclude that $B$. But this is absurd, since $B$ may be anything whatever.

**Paradox, Epimenides'** Variant of the liar paradox named after Epimenides the Cretan, who – we are to assume – asserted that all Cretans always spoke falsely. Of special interest because it does not lead to an immediate contradiction, but merely to the conclusion that on some other occasion a Cretan must have spoken truly. The contradiction lies rather in the fact that this conclusion should seemingly be derivable from the assumption when it is obviously independent of it.

**Paradox of the greatest ordinal** *See* Paradox, Burali-Forti's.

**Paradox, Grelling's** Also known as the Grelling–Nelson paradox or the paradox of heterologicality. Published in 1908 by Kurt Grelling and Leonard Nelson, it can be stated as follows. There are adjectives such as 'red' that do not apply to themselves. Call such adjectives heterological. The question then arises whether 'heterological' is heterological. If it is, then it applies to itself and so is not. On the other hand, if it is not, then it does not apply to itself and so is. Grelling and Nelson considered this a variant of Russell's paradox.

**Paradox of the heap** *See* Paradox, *sorites.*

**Paradox of heterologicality** *See* Paradox, Grelling's.

**Paradox, liar** Attributed to Eubulides (4th century BC). A man says, 'What I am saying is false'. If what he says is true then it is false, and if it is false then it is true. Assuming that it is either true or false, it follows that it must be both, which is absurd. The *strengthened* liar is a variant designed to rule out the alternative that what he says is meaningless, by having him say 'What I am saying is either false or meaningless'.

**Paradox, Richard's** First published in 1905 by Jules Richard. Consider the class *D* of non-terminating decimals that can be defined in a finite number of words. *D* can be formed into a sequence (say, by alphabetizing the verbal definitions of its elements). For every *n*, the *n*th digit of the *n*th member of this sequence can be altered according to some systematic scheme. Let the digit so altered be the *n*th digit in a new decimal *R*, the Richard decimal. *R* thus differs from every element of *D* in at least one decimal place and thus does not belong to *D*. None the less, it is a non-terminating decimal defined in a finite number of words and, so, satisfies the membership condition for *D*.

*See* Paradox, Berry's.

**Paradox, Russell's** The most celebrated of the set-theoretic paradoxes. Let *A* be the set of all sets which do not belong to themselves. If *A* belongs to itself, it must satisfy the condition for membership of *A*, that is, it must not belong to itself. This is absurd. So *A* does not belong to itself, in which case it satisfies the condition for membership of itself, which is also absurd. We have therefore to conclude that *A* does not exist. (Note that the derivation of the absurdity makes no use of the law of the excluded middle.)

*See* Axiom of comprehension; Paradox, Grelling's.

**Paradox, *sorites*** Term of logic and linguistics. Also known as the 'paradox of the heap', *soros* being Greek for heap. This refers to any of a number of paradoxical arguments related to gradual or continuous change. The most famous such argument concludes that no amount of sand constitutes a heap. This is because (1) a single grain of sand does not constitute a heap and (2) if $n$ grains of sand do not make a heap, then $n+1$ grains do not make a heap. By mathematical induction, no number of grains of sand yields a heap. Typically, *sorites* paradoxes are thought symptomatic of the vagueness of such predicates as 'heap', 'bald' and 'red'.

**Paradoxes of material and strict implication** Terms of philosophical logic, referring to some striking discrepancies between lay people's ideas about the conditional and about validity, and those favoured by the great majority of formal logicians. *Material implication* is the truth-functional surrogate for the conditional. Reading 'if' in this way produces the paradoxical result that (1) if *A* is false, or (2) if *B* is true, then every proposition of the form 'If *A*, then *B*' is true. *Strict implication* is the relation that holds between *A* and *B* if it is impossible for *A* to be true and *B* false. Logicians standardly use it as the criterion for validity of arguments, with the paradoxical result that (3) if *A* is impossible, or (4) if *B* is necessary, then every argument of the form '*A*, therefore *B*' is valid. Some (notably H.P. Grice) claim that, despite appearances, (1) and (2) are true on the ordinary conception of 'if'. Others claim that their falsity is a defect on the part of the ordinary conception, while a third party claim that their falsity shows up the limitations of mathematical logic. There is a similar division of opinion as regards (3) and (4), though the grounds are different.

**Paralogism** Term of logic. Any reasoning that is fallacious. *See* Fallacy.

**Parameter** Term of logic and mathematics generally. Signifies a quantity whose value is to be considered fixed in a given case but which varies across cases. It therefore amounts to an arbitrarily selected constant.

**Parameter theorem** *See* S-M-N theorem.

**Parametrization theorem** *See* S-M-N theorem.

**Partial function** *See* Function.

**Particular (proposition)** *See* Categorical proposition.

**Particular to general reasoning** *See* Ampliation.

**Partition** Notion of set theory. A set is partitioned when it is divided up into mutually disjunctive and exhaustive subsets. A partition on a set *A* is thus a family of subsets of *A* such that each member of *A* is an element of exactly one of these subsets. The subsets making up a partition are commonly referred to as *cells*.

*See* Equivalence class.

**Peano postulates (Peano arithmetic)** System of axioms for the arithmetic of the natural numbers. Dedekind introduced an equivalent system in 1888, but it was Peano's system introduced a year later that became widely used. In its early form, the system comprises five postulates:

(1) 0 is a natural number.

(2) Any successor of a natural number is a natural number.

(3) 0 is not the successor of any natural number.

(4) If two successors are identical, then the numbers of which they are successors are identical.

(5) For any property *P*, if (i) 0 has *P* and (ii) for any natural number *x*, if *x* has *P*, then so does the successor of *x*, then (iii) every natural number has *P*.

Formulated in this way, with a quantifier over properties in axiom (5) (the induction postulate), Peano arithmetic is a second-order system. A first-order system is obtained by treating induction not as an axiom but as an axiom schema. A modern first-order formulation of the system (now called PA) is as follows:

(A1) $\neg\exists x(0 = \mathrm{S}x)$,

(A2) $\forall x, y(\mathrm{S}x = \mathrm{S}y \rightarrow x = y)$,

(A3) $\forall x(x + 0 = x)$,

(A4) $\forall x, y(x + \mathrm{S}y = \mathrm{S}(x + y))$,

(A5) $\forall x(x \cdot 0 = 0)$,

(A6) $\forall x, y(x \cdot \mathrm{S}y = (x \cdot y) + x)$,

(AS7) For any formula $\phi$ in which $x$ does not occur bound,

$$[\phi(0)\ \&\ \forall x(\phi(x) \rightarrow \phi(\mathrm{S}x))] \rightarrow \forall x\phi(x).$$

*See* Induction, mathematical.

**Perfect syllogism** Term of traditional logic. Applied by Aristotle to the syllogisms of the first figure – Barbara, Celarent, Darii and Ferio – apparently because he believed that they were self-evidently valid, as opposed to the 'imperfect' syllogisms of the other figures, whose validity needed to be demonstrated.

*See* Figure (of a categorical syllogism); Mood (of a categorical syllogism).

***Petitio principii*** *See* Circular reasoning, fallacy of.

**Philonian conditional** *See* Conditional, material.

**Polish notation** Term of propositional logic. Notation in which the symbol for a binary connective is written before, instead of in between, the sentences it joins. The advantage is that it makes brackets unnecessary; the disadvantage, that it is difficult for some readers to follow. Example: in Polish notation

$$((p \vee q) \rightarrow \neg r) \rightarrow (r \rightarrow (\neg p \wedge \neg q))$$

is written $CCApqNrCrKNpNq$.

**Polysyllogism** An argument consisting of a sequence of syllogisms; also called '*sorites*'.

**Post completeness** Term of metalogic first introduced by the logician Emil Post. A system $T$ is said to be Post complete just in case the addition of any further statements to its set of theorems produces an inconsistent system. The usual systems of classical sentential logic are Post complete.

**Postulates, Peano** *See* Peano postulates (Peano arithmetic).

**Power (of a set)** *See* Cardinality.

**Power set** Term of set theory. The power set $\wp(A)$ of a set $A$ is the set of all subsets of $A$.

**Power set axiom** *See* Axiom of power set.

**Predecessor** Term of set theory and mathematics generally. In an ordered set, the predecessor of an element is the element which immediately precedes it when the set is arranged in order. If $x, y$ are elements of an ordered set $A$ and $y$ is less than $x$ and there is no element of $A$ which is greater than $y$ but less than $x$, then $y$ is the predecessor of $x$. If $A$ is ordered by the relation $R$, then the predecessor of $x$ in $A$ is the element $y$ such that $Ryx$ and for all $z \neq y$ if $Rzx$ then $Rzy$. 0 has no predecessor. Example: under the usual ordering of the natural numbers, the predecessor of a natural number $n$ is the number $n-1$.

*See* Discrete set; Induction, mathematical; Limit ordinal; Successor.

**Predicate** In modern logic, an expression that makes a sentence out of one or more names; also (sometimes) the relation denoted by such an expression. In traditional Aristotelian logic (as formulated in English), the predicate is the general term following the copula, as 'mortal' in 'All men are mortal'.

*See* Categorical proposition.

**Predicate-functor logic** A predicate functor, following Quine, is an expression which, when applied to predicate(s), makes another predicate. Such functors have also been called predicate modifiers or, traditionally, adverbs. Semantically, an $n$-place predicate functor maps $n$ relations into a relation. Like combinatory logic, predicate-functor logic dispenses with bound variables. The first-order predicate calculus with identity can be based entirely on predicate functors.

**Predicate logic** Branch of logic which deals with the logical features of expressions containing quantifiers and quantifiable variables. Perhaps the most basic and central such class of expressions are those containing first-order variables capable of being bound by either a *universal* quantifier or an *existential* quantifier. The logic of such expressions is commonly called *first-order predicate logic*. Higher-order predicate logics develop the logic of expressions containing higher-order quantifiable variables.

**Premise** *See* Argument.

**Prenex normal form** *See* Normal form (prenex).

**Pre-ordering** *See* Quasi-ordering.

**Primitive recursive function** *See* Recursive function.

**Principle of constructive choices** *See* Markov's principle.

**Problem** *See* Continuum hypothesis; Decision problem; Entscheidungsproblem; Halting problem; Henkin's problem; Solvable problem.

**Product (of sets)** *See* Cartesian product.

**Projection function** The $n$-ary projection function $\mathrm{P}_i^n$ (where $1 \leqslant i \leqslant n$) operates on ordered $n$-tuples and picks out the $i$th element:

$$\mathrm{P}_i^n(x_1, \ldots, x_n) = x_i.$$

*See* Recursive function.

**Proof** *See* Conditional proof; Constructive existence proof; Demonstration; Derivation; Diagonal argument; Direct proof; Formal system; *Reductio ad absurdum*.

**Proper class** *See* Class.

**Proposition** From the Middle Ages to the nineteenth century, a proposition was understood as (1) a declarative sentence considered together with its meaning or content; or as the one or the other in particular contexts. In the early twentieth century, 'proposition' came to be used in two overlapping senses: (2) the intension or meaning of a (possible) sentence; and (3) the fully determinate circumstance or content capable of being asserted or expressed by a particular utterance of a sentence. A proposition in sense (3) is the sort of thing that can be an object of belief. Sense (2) is often explicated, following Carnap, as a set of 'indices' (or a function from indices to truth-values), where an index is a possible world, a state description, a context of use, or the like. But it is not clear that this explication is adequate for all the uses to which (2) is put, for example, as what synonymous sentences have in common.

*See* Categorical proposition; Singular proposition; Syllogism, hypothetical; Validity.

**Proposition, categorical** *See* Categorical proposition.

**Propositional function** An expression or semantic entity that contains a variable or schematic name and becomes a proposition when a definite name is substituted for that variable/schematic name.

**Propositional logic** That branch of logic which deals with the logical features of propositional operators. Classically, the logic of languages whose logical expressions are truth-functional propositional operators on the two classical truth-values 'true' and 'false'.

**Propositional operator/connective** Basic notion of propositional logic. In its most general sense, a propositional operator/connective is any operator or expression of a language that forms sentences from sentences (for example, 'and', 'or', 'It is not the case that', 'Wilbur believes that'). Some of these operators are *truth-functional* in character; that is, sentences formed using them are such that their truth-values are uniquely determined by the truth-values of the component sentences. In most of their usages, the first three English operators named above are truth-functional; the fourth is not.

*See* Complete set of connectives.

**Provability predicate** A formula of the language of a theory *T* is said to be a provability predicate for *T* just in case it satisfies the derivability conditions.

*See* Derivability conditions.

# Q

**Quality (of a categorical proposition)** *See* Categorical proposition.

**Quantifier** Basic notion of logic. Classically, it referred to those syncategorematic expressions in categorical propositions (for example, 'all', 'some', 'none') that indicate the *quantity* of the proposition. In modern logic, it refers to any of a variety of operators that are capable of binding occurrences of variables so as to turn term-like expressions into terms, or propositional functions into propositions. A *universal* quantifier attached to a proposition '*A* are *B*' asserts that every element of *A* (or everything having the property *A*) is an element of (or has the property) *B*. An *existential* quantifier attached to a proposition '*A* are *B*' asserts that there is at least one element of *A* (or at least one object having the property *A*) that is an element of (or has the property) *B*.

*See* Categorical proposition; Existential generalization; Existential instantiation; Universal generalization; Universal instantiation; Variable.

**Quantity (of a categorical proposition)** *See* Categorical proposition.

**Quasi-ordering** Term of set theory and mathematics generally. *R* is a quasi-ordering (pre-ordering) on *A* iff *R* is reflexive and transitive in *A*.

*See* Relations (properties of).

# R

**Ramified theory of types** *See* Types, theory of.

**Range (of a relation/function)** Term of set theory and mathematics generally. Also referred to as the 'codomain', 'counter domain', 'converse domain' or 'right field'. For an $n$-ary relation $R$, it is the collection of elements $a_n$ for which there is an $n-1$-tuple $\langle a_1, \ldots, a_{n-1} \rangle$ such that $Ra_1 \ldots a_{n-1}a_n$. For a function $f : A \rightarrow B$ the term 'range' is used for $B$ and also for the set $\{f(x) \colon x \in A\}$ of outputs of $f$, which is a subset of B.

**Real variable** *See* Variable.

**Reasoning from particular to general** *See* Ampliation.

**Recursion theorem** Fundamental result in the theory of recursive functions, first proved by Stephen Kleene. The recursion theorem shows that the class of partial recursive functions is closed under a wide variety of inductive and implicit definitions. Here is one way of stating the theorem: whenever $f$ is a total computable function taking (Turing machine) programs into (Turing machine) programs, there is a program $P$ which is a fixed point of $f$ in the extended sense that $P$ and $f(P)$ compute precisely the same function. This result is sometimes called 'Kleene's second recursion theorem', to distinguish it from another, related 'first recursion theorem' also proved by Kleene.

*See* Recursive function; Turing machine.

**Recursive function** Term of computability theory. A function on the natural numbers is recursive if it is one of the following:

(1) the identity function, a constant function, the successor

function or a projection function;

(2) definable by composition of recursive functions;

(3) definable from recursive functions by recursion;

(4) definable in terms of a given recursive function $\phi$ as the least natural number such that $\phi$ takes the value zero.

A function is *primitive recursive* if it is definable using only (1)–(3). A primitive recursive function must be *total*, that is, defined for every natural number (or $n$-tuple, for appropriate $n$) as input. Moreover, the function which gives the number of steps required to calculate the value for any input is computable. A recursive function need not be total since the recursive function in terms of which it is defined in (4) above might never take the value zero. It is not in general decidable whether a given recursive function is total; even if it is total, there need not be any computable bound to the number of steps required to calculate its value. The recursive functions can be proved to coincide with the Turing computable functions, and with those computable by register machines. Church's thesis is the claim that these classes of functions coincide with those which are computable algorithmically.

*See* Computable function; Recursion theorem; Turing computable function.

**Recursive set** Term of computability theory. A set of natural numbers is said to be recursive if the characteristic function of the set is total recursive. Church's thesis claims that the recursive sets are just the decidable ones.

*See* Decidability; Recursive function.

**Recursively enumerable set** Term of computability theory. A set of natural numbers is recursively enumerable if it is the range of a recursive function or, equivalently, if the characteristic function of the set is partial recursive. If Church's thesis holds, the recursively enumerable sets are just the semi-decidable ones.

*See* Decidability; Recursive function.

**Reducibility, axiom of** *See* Axiom of reducibility.

***Reductio absurdum*** Term of logic. This is the rule, valid in most systems of logic, that if you can deduce a contradictory pair of sentences *q*, not-*q* from an assumption *p*, then *p* must be false and not-*p* (the contradictory of *p*) follows. When *p* is itself negative, the rule is also called indirect proof. *Reductio ad absurdum* (or *reductio ad impossibile*) was a mode of immediate inference in Aristotle's syllogistic.

*See* Immediate inference.

**Reduction, syllogistic** Aristotle's derivation of all categorical syllogisms from the first figure with the help of some immediate (one-premise) inferences. Aristotle considered the four syllogistic moods of the first figure to be axiomatic, but he also showed that the moods of the second figure or the third figure could serve equally well as axioms. Thus Aristotle gave three different axiomatizations of categorical syllogistic.

*See* Figure (of a categorical syllogism); Perfect syllogism.

**Reflexive relation/order** *See* Relations (properties of).

**Register machine** Concept of computability theory. A register machine is a type of automaton or idealized computing device characterizing computable functions, closely related to the notion of an abacus machine. It consists of an infinite array of abstract memory locations or registers and a finite set of simple instructions for the stepwise manipulation of data stored in these registers. A numerical function is register computable just in case there is a register program which computes its outputs correctly from its inputs using the set of registers. It is provable that a function is register computable precisely when it is Turing computable or, equivalently, recursive.

*See* Computable function; Recursive function; Turing computable function.

**Regularity, axiom of** *See* Axiom of foundation.

**Relation** Notion of logic and set theory. In the first systematic treatment by De Morgan, relations were treated as generalized copulae. De Morgan defined a proposition to be the presentation of two names under a relation, and took its general form to be '$s$ is in relation $R$ to $p$', with $R$ acting as a copula between the subject $s$ and the predicate $p$. He treated relational expressions as having both *intensions* and *extensions.* He also saw a general theory of relations as having to allow for relational expressions with any finite number of terms or *arguments.* Modern logic takes the extension of an $n$-termed relational expression to be a set of $n$-tuples of elements of the set on which the relation is defined, known as the *field* of the relation.

*See* Ancestral (of a relation); Arity; Converse (of a relation); Domain (of a relation/function); Equivalence relation; Field (of a relation/function); Function; Ordering; Predicate; Predicate-functor logic; Range (of a relation/function); Relations (properties of); Well-ordering.

**Relations (properties of)** Let $R$ be a relation on a set $A$. Then:

$R$ is *connected* (or *complete*) in $A$ iff any two distinct elements of $A$ are $R$-related: for any $x, y$ in $A$, then $Rxy$ (read: '$x$ bears $R$ to $y$') or $Ryx$ or $x = y$.

$R$ is *strongly* connected iff for any $x, y$ in $A$, either $Rxy$ or $Ryx$.

$R$ is *dense* iff whenever $R$ relates two elements of $A$ there is a third which relates to both of them as follows: if $Rxy$, there is a $z$ in $A$ such that $Rxz$ and $Rzy$.

$R$ is *reflexive* iff $R$ relates every element of $A$ to itself: $Rxx$ for every $x$ in $A$.

$R$ is *irreflexive* iff no element of $A$ is $R$-related to itself: if $Rxy$ then $x \neq y$.

$R$ is *symmetric* iff $R$ and its converse coincide: for all $x, y$ in $A$, if $Rxy$, then $Ryx$.

$R$ is *antisymmetric* iff no two distinct elements of $A$ are in both $R$ and its converse: if $Rxy$ and $Ryx$ then $x = y$.

$R$ is *asymmetric* iff for any $x,y$ in $A$ if $Rxy$, then not $Ryx$.

$R$ is *transitive* iff whenever $R$ relates $x$ to $y$ and $y$ to $z$, then it relates $x$ directly to $z$: if $Rxy$ and $Ryz$, then $Rxz$.

$R$ is *linear* (or *simple* or *total*) in $A$ iff $R$ is antisymmetric, connected, reflexive and transitive in $A$.

$R$ is *well-founded* iff every non-empty subset of $A$ has a least element under $R$: for all $B \subset A$, if $B \neq \emptyset$ then there is a unique $b$ in $B$ such that for every $x$ in $A$, if $x \neq b$ then $Rbx$; in other words, there are no infinite descending chains of $R$-related elements.

If $A$ is ordered by a relation $R$ having any of the above properties, then $R$ is said to be an *order(ing)* of that type on $A$. There is some variation concerning the definitions of the above terms.

*See* Converse (of a relation); Ordering; Well-ordering.

**Relative complement** *See* Complement.

**Replacement, axiom of** *See* Axiom of replacement.

**Restriction, axiom of** *See* Axiom of foundation.

**Richard's paradox** *See* Paradox, Richard's.

**Right field (of a relation)** *See* Range (of a relation/function).

**Rules of inference** *See* Inference.

**Russell's paradox** *See* Paradox, Russell's.

# S

**Satisfaction** Basic concept of model theory and formal semantics, introduced by Tarski in order to define truth for languages with quantifiers. It signifies a three-place relation between (a) formulae of a formal language *L*, (b) interpretations or structures *M* for *L*, and (c) sequences of items from the domain of *M*. Intuitively, a sequence satisfies a formula under an interpretation just in case the formula, so interpreted, holds of the items of the sequence taken in the order in which the sequence arranges them. Thus, for example, if $m_1$ and $m_2$ are elements of the domain of *M* and '*Rxy*' is a formula of *L*, the sequence $\langle m_1, m_2 \rangle$ satisfies '*Rxy*' under *M* just in case $\langle m_1, m_2 \rangle$ is in the extension (i.e. the set of ordered pairs of elements of the domain of *M*) assigned to '*Rxy*' by *M*. Sentences (i.e. formulas containing no occurrences of free variables) turn out to be satisfied by all sequences under *M* if they are satisfied by any. A sentence that is satisfied by all (some) sequences under *M* is said to be true-in-*M*. A set *S* of sentences of *L* is said to be satisfiable (or simultaneously satisfiable) just in case there is at least one structure *M* for *L* that makes all the sentences in *S* true.

*See* Interpretation; Structure.

**Sentence** Term of logic. In a formal language, a formula is said to be a sentence if it contains no free occurrences of variables.

*See* Variable.

**Separation, axiom of** *See* Axiom of separation.

**Sequence** Notion of set theory and mathematics generally. A sequence is an ordered set of objects that is either finite or countably infinite and thus indexable by the natural numbers or some initial segment of them.

**Sequent systems, rules of** *See* Contraction; Dilution.

**Series** Term of mathematics generally. Sometimes used as a synonym for sequence. Strictly speaking, however, a series is the sum of a sequence of terms.

**Set/class distinction** *See* Von Neumann–Bernays–Gödel set theory.

**Set theory** *See* Von Neumann–Bernays–Gödel set theory; Zermelo–Fraenkel set theory.

**Set-theoretic axioms** *See* Axioms, set-theoretic.

**Sheffer stroke** *See* Alternative denial.

**Signature** Notion of model theory. The signature of a structure or model $M$ is specified by giving (1) the set of individual constants to which $M$ assigns elements of its domain, (2) for each $n > 0$, the set of $n$-ary relation symbols to which $M$ assigns sets of $n$-tuples of elements of its domain as extensions, and (3) for each $n > 0$, the set of $n$-ary function symbols to which $M$ assigns sets of $n+1$-tuples of elements of its domain as extensions. 'Signature' is another term for what model theorists often refer to as a 'language', by which they mean not a whole formal language (complete with logical symbols, such devices as parentheses and a grammar), but rather those elements of a formal language whose different interpretation serves to differentiate models or structures that have the same domain.

*See* Structure.

**Signification** From the Latin for 'to make a sign'. Signification, in common use, refers variously to the meaning of something (in a very general sense), to acts of assigning a meaning and to the creation of symbols. In medieval logic and semantics, '*significatio*' was the standard meaning of a sign or some special aspect of that meaning. From the late twelfth century, '*significatio*' was standardly counted among the four major properties of terms and referred to the meaning of a term or to its range of ordinary uses.

**Similarity (of ordered sets)** *See* Order type.

**Simple relation/order** *See* Relations (properties of).

**Simple theory of types** *See* Types, theory of.

**Singular proposition** Term of logic. In modern logic a singular proposition is a simple sentence consisting of nothing but a predicate and the appropriate number of singular terms, as '*Fa*' or '*Rxy*'. Traditionally, a singular proposition is a categorical proposition with a proper name as subject term. No express quantifier is present, but William of Ockham construed the proper name as a universally quantified term of unit extension, thereby rendering singular propositions tractable in syllogistic.

*See* Categorical proposition.

**Skolem theorem** *See* Löwenheim–Skolem theorem(s).

**Skolem normal form** *See* Normal form (Skolem).

**S-M-N theorem** Fundamental result of computability theory, also known as the 'parametrization theorem' or 'parameter theorem', first proved by Stephen Kleene. In general, the theorem states that, given a multi-input computable function, each of the functions obtained from it by fixing several of its inputs as parameters is also computable and a program for the latter (say, a Turing machine program) can be found effectively from the parameters and a program for the original function. In the case of a binary computable function $f(x,y)$, this means that there is an algorithmic method $M$ which, given a program $P$ for $f$ and any number $n$, finds a program for the parametrized function of $y$, $f(n,y)$, that we get by fixing the value of $x$ at $n$ and letting $y$ vary. The title derives from Kleene's notation for the method $M$.

**Solvable problem** Basic notion in computability theory. A problem is an infinite set of numerical or mathematical questions of the form 'Does $x$ have property $P$?' where $x$ is variable, such as 'Is number $n$ even?' and 'Is $A$ a theorem of predicate logic?'. A problem is solvable or recursively solvable when there is an algorithmic procedure which supplies correct yes-or-no answers to all of the specific questions posed by the problem. Otherwise, the problem is said to be (recursively) unsolvable. In other words, a problem 'Does *x* have property *P*?' is solvable when there is an effective procedure which, given any suitable value *n* for *x*, will compute a correct answer to the specific question 'Does *n* have *P*?'. Examples: the problems 'Does Turing machine program *P* halt on any input?' and 'Is *A* a theorem of full predicate logic?' are recursively unsolvable.

*See* Algorithm; Church's theorem; Decision problem; Entscheidungsproblem; Halting problem.

**Sophism** Term used by Aristotle (*Topics*, 162a14) to describe an argument that is not valid but may misleadingly appear to be so.

***Sorites*** *See* Paradox, *sorites*; Polysyllogism.

**Soundness (of an argument)** Term of basic logic. An argument is said to be sound when it is valid and all its premises are true.

*See* Validity.

**Soundness (of a formal system)** Term of metalogic. A formal system or calculus is said to be sound when all its theorems or derivations have the property (typically semantic) that the system is supposed to formalize. An arithmetic formalism is said to be sound when all its theorems are truths of arithmetic.

*See* Soundness (of a logical calculus).

**Soundness (of a logical calculus)** Term of metalogic. A logical calculus is *weakly* sound if every logical theorem is a logical truth. If one is interested in formalizing the more general notion of logical consequence, then one will require that the calculus is also *strongly* sound, that is, whenever a sentence $S$ can be derived from a set of premises $\Gamma$, $S$ is a logical consequence of $\Gamma$.

*See* Completeness (of a logical calculus).

**Soundness (of a theory)** Term of metamathematics. A theory is sound if each of its theorems is true in the intended structure. Example: every theorem of first-order Peano arithmetic is true in the intended structure of the natural numbers.

*See* Theory.

**Square of opposition** *See* Opposition.

**Strengthened liar paradox** *See* Paradox, liar.

**Strict implication** *See* Paradoxes of material and strict implication.

**Structure** Central notion of model theory. A structure $M$ for a language (or signature) $L$ is a pair $\langle D, I \rangle$, where $D$ is a set referred to as the domain of $M$ (sometimes also called the universe of discourse of $M$ or the carrier of $M$) and $I$ (called the interpretation function of $M$) is a function which maps each individual constant of $L$ to an element of $D$, each $n$-ary relation of $L$ to a set of $n$-tuples of elements of $D$, and each m-ary function of $L$ to a mapping of the m-tuples of elements of $D$ to the elements of $D$. A structure is a *model* of a theory (that is, a set of sentences) $T$ when it makes every element of $T$ true. Classically, $D$ is required to be non-empty, though this requirement is no longer enforced as a general requirement in model-theoretic work.

*See* Interpretation; Nonstandard model; Satisfaction; Signature.

**Subalternation** The subaltern of 'All *A* are *B*' is 'Some *A* are *B*'; and that of 'No *A* are *B*' is 'Some *A* are not *B*'. Subalternation, the immediate inference to the subaltern, is recognized as valid in Aristotelian and traditional logic. Its validity depends upon the existential assumption that there are *A*s. Syllogisms provable (reducible) with the help of subalternation are called subaltern syllogisms.

*See* Immediate inference.

**Subcontradictories** *See* Opposition.

**Subject** The thing a statement is about; its topic. Subject term (or just 'subject'): the term referring to the subject. In modern logic, a subject term is a singular term in an atomic sentence. In traditional Aristotelian logic, the subject term of a categorical proposition is the general term following the quantifier, as 'men' in 'All men are mortal.'

*See* Categorical proposition.

**Subjunctive conditional** *See* Conditional, counterfactual.

**Subset** Terms of set theory. $A$ is a subset of $B$ iff every element of $A$ is also an element of $B$. In this case, $B$ is also referred to as a *superset* of $A$. $A$ is a *proper* subset of $B$ iff $A$ is a subset of $B$ and $B$ contains some element that is not an element of $A$. In this case $B$ is referred to as a proper superset of $A$. More generally, if $D$ is any collection, $A$ is said to be a subset of $B$ with respect to $D$ iff every element of $D$ that is an element of $A$ is also an element of $B$.

**Substitution, axiom of** *See* Axiom of replacement.

**Subtheory** *See* Extension (of a theory).

**Successor** Term of set theory and mathematics generally. In an ordered set, the successor of an element is the element which immediately succeeds it when the set is arranged in order. If $x, y$ are elements of an ordered set $A$, and $y$ is greater than $x$ and there is no element of $A$ which is less than $y$ but greater than $x$, then $y$ is the successor of $x$, often written as $x'$. If $A$ is ordered by the relation $R$, then the successor of $x$ in $A$ is the element $x'$ such that $Rxx'$ and for all $y \neq x'$ if $Rxy$ then $Rx'y$. Example: under the usual ordering of the natural numbers, the successor of a natural number $n$ is the number $n+1$.

*See* Discrete set; Induction, mathematical; Limit ordinal; Peano postulates (Peano arithmetic); Predecessor; Successor.

**Successor function** The successor function maps every element to its successor: for all $x$, $S(x)=x'$.

*See* Recursive function.

**Sumset axiom** *See* Axiom of union.

**Superset** *See* Subset.

***Supremum*** *See* Bound (of a set).

**Surjection** *See* Onto function.

**Syllogism** *See* Antilogism; Categorical proposition; Conversion *per accidens*; Conversion, simple; Dilemma; Distributed term (of a syllogism); Enthymeme; Existential import; Figure (of a categorical syllogism); Immediate inference; Major premise (of a syllogism); Major term (of a syllogism); Middle term (of a syllogism); Minor premise (of a syllogism); Minor term (of a syllogism); Mnemonics, syllogistic; *Modus ponendo tollens*; *Modus ponens*; *Modus tollendo ponens*; *Modus tollens*; Mood (of a categorical syllogism); Opposition; Perfect syllogism; Polysyllogism; *Reductio ad absurdum*; Reduction, syllogistic; Singular proposition; Subalternation; Syllogism, categorical; Syllogism, disjunctive; Syllogism, hypothetical; Syllogism, modal.

**Syllogism, categorical** A valid form of argument in the oldest known system of formal logic in the West, presented by Aristotle at the beginning of his *Prior Analytics.* A syllogistic argument has a major premise, a minor premise and a conclusion, all of them categorical propositions. (Hence the name ‘categorical syllogism’; hypothetical syllogisms consist of compound propositions.)

*See* Categorical proposition.

**Syllogism, disjunctive** Originally, this referred to either of the two valid argument forms '*p* or *q*;*p*; therefore not *q*' (the 'fourth indemonstrable' of Stoic logic) or '*p* or *q*; not *p*; therefore *q*' (the 'fifth indemonstrable'), or the same but with the major premise commuted. The 'or' here was exclusive. The disjunctive syllogism was considered a species of hypothetical syllogism. Now 'disjunctive syllogism' is used only for the second form (corresponding to the fifth indemonstrable), but with 'or' taken inclusively. It fails in certain relevance logics.

**Syllogism, horned** *See* Dilemma.

**Syllogism, hypothetical** Originally, this referred to a valid two-premise argument from conditionals; later involving various connectives. Aristotle's syllogisms consist of categorical propositions but he also spoke of 'syllogisms from hypotheses'. Theophrastus was credited with formulating hypothetical syllogisms, particularly 'thoroughly hypothetical syllogisms', such as 'If *A* then *B*; if *B* then *C*; so if *A* then *C*'. This is what is called 'hypothetical syllogism' today. (By the time of Boethius, the term had been extended to Stoic two-premise arguments in general.)

**Syllogism, modal** A two-premise argument made up of modalized and unmodalized categorical propositions. For Aristotle the modalization typically affected the predicate term: for example, 'All *A* are necessarily-*B*'. Thus the modality was *de re.* He recognized both one-sided possibility ('not impossible') and two-sided possibility (contingency). His most curious form of modalized categorical proposition was 'All possibly-*A* are possibly-*B*', and similarly for other quantities and qualities (two-sided possibility). Theophrastus interpreted the modalities *de dicto*, which gave much clearer results. Ultimately, the two systems complement each other. Example: 'All men are necessarily animals; all Greeks are men; so all Greeks are necessarily animals'.

*See* Categorical proposition.

**Syllogism, perfect** *See* Perfect syllogism.

**Symmetric difference of sets** *See* Difference of sets.

**Symmetric relation/order** *See* Relations (properties of).

**Syncategoremata** Term of traditional logic. Signifies a term which cannot serve as a subject or predicate term of a categorical proposition, such as adverbs and conjunctions. Contrasted with categoremata. Examples: 'all', 'if', 'and'.

*See* Categoremata.

**Synthetic (judgment or proposition)** *See* Analytic/synthetic (judgment or proposition).

# T

**Tarski's undefinability theorem** Basic theorem proved by Tarski in 1936 concerning the definability of the notion of truth in formal languages. It states that there is no formula in the language of arithmetic true of all and only the Gödel numbers of the truths of arithmetic.

**Tautology, tautological implication** Basic notions of logic. A proposition is said to be a tautology when its truth is logically necessary or, equivalently, when its negation is a contradiction. A sentence built up by means of truth-functional operators is a tautology if it is true under every assignment of truth-values to the atomic sentences. A set of premises tautologically imply a conclusion if every assignment of truth-values to the atomic sentences that make all the premises true also makes the conclusion true. Examples: '$p \vee \neg p$' is a tautology; '$p$' and '$p \rightarrow q$' tautologically imply '$q$'.

**T-equivalence** Notion of Tarskian semantics. Signifies a sentence of the form '[*S*] is true iff *S*', where the letter '*S*' stands for a sentence of a given language *L* and '[*S*]' stands for some name of that sentence in *L*. Tarski maintained that any materially (that is, extensionally) adequate definition of truth for *L* would have to satisfy all the *T*-equivalences formulable in *L*.

***Tertium non datur*** *See* Law of (the) excluded middle.

**Theorem** *See* Cantor's theorem; Church's theorem; Completeness theorem; Cut-elimination theorems; De Morgan's laws; Deduction theorem; Herbrand's theorem; Incompleteness theorems; Löb's theorem; Löwenheim–Skolem theorem(s); Markov's principle; Recursion theorem; S-M-N theorem; Tarski's undefinability theorem.

**Theory** Term of metamathematics. A (formal) theory is a set *T* of sentences (or formulas) of a formal language that is closed under logical consequence, that is, *T* is such that everything that follows from members of *T* is also in *T*. The elements of *T* are its *theorems*. Examples: a set of axioms together with all their consequences is a theory. The set of all the sentences true in a structure *M* is a theory.

*See* Axiomatic theory.

**Theory, axiomatic** *See* Axiomatic theory.

**Theory, categorical** *See* Categorical theory.

**Theory, completeness of a** *See* Completeness (of a theory).

**Theory, (conservative) extension of a** *See* Extension (of a theory).

**Theory, soundness of a** *See* Soundness (of a theory).

**Theory of types** *See* Types, theory of.

**Thinning** *See* Dilution.

**Total function** *See* Function.

**Total relation/order** *See* Ordering; Relations (properties of).

**Transfinite cardinal** Term of set theory. A cardinal number is transfinite when it represents the size of some infinite set. In many developments of set theory, a cardinal number is transfinite when it cannot be put into one-one correspondence with any finite set. Examples: $\aleph_0$ and all larger cardinals are transfinite.

**Transfinite induction** Concept of set theory. Transfinite induction, a generalization of ordinary, finite mathematical induction, is one or another principle of inductive proof as applied to an ordinal number or well-ordered set which is larger than that of the natural numbers. Generally, transfinite induction on a well-ordered set *A* shows that every element of

*A* has a property *P* by proving that, whenever all the order predecessors of an element *x* in *A* have *P*, then so does *x*.

*See* Induction, mathematical.

**Transitive closure** *See* Ancestral (of a relation).

**Transitive relation/order** *See* Relations (properties of).

**Trichotomy** *See* Law of trichotomy.

**Truth-function** Term of formal propositional logic. A truth-function takes (lists of) truth-values into truth-values. In classical, two-valued logic, a truth-function takes *n*-tuples of elements of the set {T, F} to the set {T, F}. In many-valued logics, truth-functions take their arguments and values from larger sets. Generally speaking, if there are *k* different basic truth-values, there are $k^n$ *n*-ary truth-functions.

*See* Truth-value.

**Truth in a model** *See* Satisfaction.

**Truth table** Basic notion of propositional logic. A truth table is a diagram displaying, for a propositional formula or argument, the truth-values of the whole formula or argument as determined by each possible combination of the truth-values of its ultimate constituents (frequently referred to as 'base components' or 'atomic sentences'). In a logic with *k* different basic truth-values, a proposition made up of *n* atomic sentences, or an *n*-ary truth-function, is given by a truth table that has *n* input columns and one output column, each of $k^n$ rows. Example:

| $A$ | $B$ | $A \wedge B$ |
|---|---|---|
| T | T | T |
| T | F | F |
| F | T | F |
| F | F | F |

*See* Truth-value.

**Truth-value** Term of formal propositional logic. In classical, two-valued logic, the members of the set {T, F}, 'true' and 'false', are conventionally adopted as truth-values, that is, objects over which propositional formulas are interpreted. For nonclassical and many-valued logics, other sets of truth-values provide objects for interpretation. Sometimes, elements of Boolean algebras or open sets from topological spaces serve as useful sets of truth-values.

**-Tuple** Term of set theory and mathematics generally. An *n*-tuple is a set of *n* elements. An *ordered n*-tuple is a set of *n* elements in a particular arrangement in which the position of an element is meaningful, in addition to its presence.

**Turing computable function** Term of computability theory. A function with natural number inputs and outputs is Turing computable when there is a Turing machine which computes its correct outputs, given its inputs. More precisely, *f* is Turing computable when there is a Turing machine which, when given a number *n* for which *f* gives a value, eventually computes that value and which, when given a number for which *f* does not yield a value, never ceases computation and, so, never produces an output. Alan Turing introduced the notion of a function computed by a Turing machine in proving the undecidability of first-order logic. According to Church's thesis, the Turing computable functions coincide precisely with those which are mechanically computable in an intuitive sense. The Turing computable functions can be proved to coincide with those which are recursive and those which are computable by register machines.

*See* Church's thesis; Computable function; Recursive function; Turing machine.

**Turing machine** Notion fundamental to computability theory. Devised by Turing as a characterization of the notion of computable function or mechanical calculation, a Turing machine is an abstract automaton or idealized computing device which consists of a program – a finite set of simple instructions – to be carried out on a one-dimensional recording tape by a reading-writing device with a memory restricted in capacity. A numerical function *f* is said to be computed by a Turing machine or to be Turing computable just in case there is a program which, when implemented, mimics on its tape the input-output behaviour of *f*. Turing computability can be proved to be equivalent to register computability and to a function's being recursive.

*See* Computable function; Recursion theorem; Recursive function; Register machine; Turing computable function.

**Types, theory of** A foundational theory devised by Russell and Whitehead to provide a way around the paradoxes of set theory. Russell believed the paradoxes to arise from the use of assumptions to the effect that classes and their members do not need to be distinguished in such a way as to prohibit reference to a set containing an object in the definition of that object. His simple theory of types stratified the universe of objects into levels or types. The lowest type contains only individuals. The next level is comprised of collections of individuals, the next collections of collections of individuals, and so on. In general, collections are formed exclusively of elements taken from the immediately preceding type. Russell provided a more complex stratification scheme in his ramified theory of types.

# U

**Union, axiom of** *See* Axiom of union.

**Union (of sets)** Notion of set theory. Given sets $A$ and $B$, their union $A \cup B$ is the set containing just those things that are either elements of $A$ or elements of $B$ (or both).

**Universal generalization** Rule governing the logic of the universal quantifier. It permits one to conclude that everything has the property $P$ from a premise to the effect that an arbitrarily selected object $o$ has $P$. In saying that $o$ is arbitrarily selected, we mean that one has no information about it that could serve to distinguish it from any other object. It thus functions as a kind of generic object.

**Universal instantiation** Rule governing the logic of the universal quantifier. It permits one to conclude of any object $o$ that it has the property $P$ from the premise that everything has $P$.

**Universal machine theorem** *See* Universal Turing machine.

**Universal (proposition)** *See* Categorical proposition.

**Universal quantifier** *See* Quantifier.

**Universal set** Term of set theory. Signifies the set of everything. Most modern set theories do not allow a universal set.

**Universal Turing machine** The 'universal machine theorem' is an important result in computability theory, first proved by Alan Turing. It asserts, in the case of Turing machines, that there are special, 'universal' Turing machines which will, given a numerical representation of an arbitrary machine program $P$ and suitable inputs $n$ for $P$, mimic the behaviour of $P$ on $n$ and compute the result $P$ would have computed when given *n*. One might say that a universal Turing machine is an abstract version of a contemporary stored-program computer. Similar universal machine theorems are provable for alternative machine-theoretic characterizations of the recursive functions, for example, register machines.

*See* Register machine; Turing machine.

**Upper bound** *See* Bound (of a set).

**Upward Löwenheim–Skolem theorem** *See* Löwenheim–Skolem theorem(s).

# V

**Validity** Basic notion of logic. In modern usage, it is applied both to arguments or inferences and to individual propositions. It is also traditionally divided into two types, *deductive* and *inductive*, although some would reserve it for the deductive case alone. In the deductive case, an *argument* is valid if it is impossible that all the premises be true and the conclusion false; a *proposition* is valid if it is impossible that the proposition be false. In the inductive case, an argument is valid if the premises being true makes it likely (to some implied degree) that the conclusion is true.

*See* Church's theorem; Paradoxes of material and strict implication.

**Valuation** Term of mathematical logic and formal semantics. Generally, a valuation for a formal language, given a semantic domain *D*, is any function which assigns appropriate semantic values over *D* to chosen expressions of the language. In predicate logic, 'valuation' often refers to functions (also called 'assignments') from the set of variables of a language into the universe of a structure *D*. Occasionally, 'valuation' is used as a synonym for 'interpretation'.

*See* Interpretation.

**Value (of a function)** *See* Function.

**Variable** Term of logic. A variable is a linguistic expression, typically a letter of the alphabet, having, in the context, no fixed, determined value but capable of adopting any of a range of values. Variables are often said to 'range over' items in those domains in which they are assigned values. In many formalisms, not all appearances of variables in a well-formed expression need be attached to a binding operator (for example, a quantifier); those which are are called 'bound'

(Russell: 'apparent'), and those which are not are called 'free' (Russell: 'real'). An *open* term or formula is one that contains some free occurrence of a quantifiable variable. Types in a hierarchy of systems or languages are often distinguished by the order of the variables available.

*See* First-order/higher-order; Sentence; Types, theory of.

**Vicious-circle principle** *See* Impredicative definition.

**Von Neumann–Bernays–Gödel set theory** Axiomatization of set theory, introduced in 1925 by John von Neumann and further developed, first, by Paul Bernays and, later, by Gödel. The two leading ideas of von Neumann–Bernays–Gödel set theory (NBG) are: first, the distinction between classes and sets. In other words, the NBG axioms refer both to classes – collections of all items having a common property – and sets, classes which can be members of other classes. The second leading idea, called limitation of size, is embodied in the principle that a class is a set provided that it is not too big. More specifically, this means that a class is a set when it is incapable of one-to-one correspondence with the collection of all sets. The conventional formulation of NBG has finitely many axioms for sets and classes: comprehension, extensionality (for classes), foundation, infinity, pairing, power set, replacement and union.

*See* Zermelo–Fraenkel set theory.

**Weakening** *See* Dilution.

**Well-founded relation/order** *See* Relations (properties of).

**Well-ordering** Term of set theory and mathematics generally. A set $A$ is well-ordered by a relation $R$ (equivalently, $R$ is a well-ordering of $A$) just in case $R$ is an ordering of $A$ and every non-empty subset of $A$ has an $R$-least element.

*See* Ordering; Relations (properties of).

# Z

**Zermelo–Fraenkel set theory** A theory intended to capture basic Cantorean principles of sets while avoiding known set-theoretic paradoxes, axioms for which were first proposed by Ernst Zermelo in 1908 and further developed by Abraham Fraenkel, Thoralf Skolem and Hermann Weyl, among others. Popularly, Zermelo–Fraenkel set theory (ZF) is standardly presented with axioms of extensionality, foundation, infinity, pairing, power set, replacement, separation and union; it is often extended – to the theory ZFC – by adding the axiom of choice. The guiding idea of ZF is a conception of set as 'iterative', on which all sets appear within a single cumulative hierarchy, divided into stages by ordinal numbers, each stage obtained via the power set operation from preceding stages.

*See* Forcing; Von Neumann–Bernays–Gödel set theory.

**Zorn's lemma** A noted maximality principle of set theory first introduced by Hausdorff in 1909; rediscovered by Zorn in 1933. Zorn's lemma asserts that a non-empty partially ordered set has a maximal element provided that each totally ordered subcollection of its members is bounded above. Zorn's lemma is provably equivalent to the axiom of choice in standard set theories and is extremely useful in a wide variety of formal contexts, among them proofs for completeness.

*See* Axiom of choice; Ordering.

# Table of logical symbols

*Set theory*

|  |  |
|---|---|
| $\{x\colon Px\}$<br>$\{x\mid Px\}$<br>$\hat{x}Px$ | Set abstraction (read: 'the set of things $x$ such that $x$ has $P$') |
| $x \in A$ | Membership ('$x$ is an element of $A$') |
| $A \subseteq B$<br>$A \subset B$ | Subset ('$A$ is a subset of $B$') |
| $A \subset B$<br>$A \subsetneqq B$ | Proper subset |
| $A \supseteq B$<br>$A \supset B$ | Superset ('$A$ is a superset of $B$') |
| $A \supset B$<br>$A \supsetneqq B$ | Proper superset |
| $\bar{A}$<br>$A'$<br>$-A$ | Complement of $A$ |
| $A_1 \times \ldots \times A_n$ | Cartesian product of $A_1, \ldots, A_n$ |
| $A - B$<br>$A \setminus B$ | Difference of $A$ and $B$ |
| $A \oplus B$<br>$A \triangle B$ | Symmetric difference of $A$ and $B$ |
| $A \cap B$<br>$AB$ | Intersection (meet, logical product) of $A$ and $B$ |

| | |
|---|---|
| $\bigcap \gamma$<br>$\bigcap_{\alpha \in \gamma} \alpha$ | Intersection of the family of sets $\gamma$ |
| $A \cup B$<br>$A + B$ | Union (join, logical sum) of $A$ and $B$ |
| $\bigcup \gamma$<br>$\bigcup_{\alpha \in \gamma} \alpha$ | Union of the family of sets $\gamma$ |
| $\mathbf{V}$<br>$1$ | The universal set |
| $\Lambda$<br>$0$<br>$\emptyset$ | The empty set |
| $(a,b)$<br>$\langle a,b \rangle$ | Ordered pair of $a$ and $b$ |
| $\{a,b\}$ | Unordered pair of $a$ and $b$ |
| $A \simeq B$ | Equipollence ('$A$ is equipollent to $B$') |
| $A \upharpoonleft R$ | Relation $R$ with its domain restricted to $A$ |
| $R \upharpoonright A$ | Relation $R$ with its converse domain restricted to $A$ |
| $R \upharpoonleft\!\upharpoonright A$ | Relation $R$ with its field restricted to $A$ |
| $\breve{R}$<br>$R^{-1}$ | Converse (inverse) of relation $R$ |

*Propositional and predicate logic*

| | |
|---|---|
| $\forall x$<br>$(x)$<br>$\Pi x$<br>$\wedge x$ | Universal quantifier ('for all $x \ldots$') |

| Symbols | Meaning |
|---|---|
| $\exists x$<br>$(\mathrm{E}x)$<br>$\Sigma x$<br>$\bigvee x$ | Existential quantifier ('there exists $x$ . . .') |
| $\iota x$ | Definite description operator ('the unique $x$ . . .') |
| $p \rightarrow q$<br>$p \supset q$<br>$Cpq$ | Conditional ('$p$ implies $q$') |
| $p \leftarrow q$<br>$Bpq$ | Inverse conditional |
| $p \leftrightarrow q$<br>$p \equiv q$<br>$Epq$<br>$p \sim q$ | Biconditional ('$p$ if and only if $q$') |
| $\neg p$<br>$\sim p$<br>$Np$<br>$-p$<br>$p'$<br>$\bar{p}$ | Negation ('not $p$') |
| $p \,\&\, q$<br>$p \wedge q$<br>$Kpq$<br>$pq$<br>$p \cdot q$ | Conjunction ('$p$ and $q$') |

|  |  |
|---|---|
| $p \vee q$, $Apq$ | Disjunction (inclusive) (‘*p* or *q* [or both]’) |
| $p \veebar q$, $Jpq$ | Disjunction (exclusive) (‘*p* or *q* [but not both]’) |
| $p \downarrow q$, $Xpq$ | Joint denial (‘neither *p* nor *q*’) |
| $p \mid q$, $Dpq$ | Alternative denial (Sheffer stroke) (‘not both *p* and *q*’) |
| $\top$ | Verum (the constant true truth-function) |
| $\bot$ | Falsum (the constant false truth-function) |
| $=$ | Identity (a logical constant) |
| $\neq$ | Difference |
| $\therefore$, $/$ | Therefore |

*Modal logic*

|  |  |
|---|---|
| $\Box p$, $Np$, $Lp$ | Necessity (‘it is necessary that *p*’) |
| $\Diamond p$, $Mp$ | Possibility (‘it is possible that *p*’) |
| $p \prec q$ | Strict implication (‘*p* strictly implies *q*’) |
| $p \circ q$ | Compossibility (‘*p* and *q* are jointly possible’) |

*Metalogic*

| | |
|---|---|
| $\Gamma \vdash A$ | $A$ is formally deducible from the set of sentences $\Gamma$ |
| $\vdash A$ | $A$ is a logical theorem |
| $\Gamma \models A$ | $A$ is a logical consequence of the set of sentences $\Gamma$ |
| $\models A$ | $A$ is a logical truth |
| $\models_M A$ | $A$ is true in structure (model) $M$ |
| $A \Rightarrow B$ | Implication (used informally) ('$A$ implies $B$') |